Nils Stripey Top
in Midnight (101) and Snow (124)
pattern on page 42

From left to right: **Lovisa Cardigan**
in Storm (102), Putty Grey (121) and
Fuchsia (143) pattern on page 92
and **Charlotte Cardigan** in Putty Grey (121)
pattern on page 12

CONTENTS

INTRODUCTION

Welcome to Wonderland – our journey through an enchanted forest, via a surreal Fair Isle fantasy to a magical tea party. We wanted to create a collection of knitting designs that captured the sense of fun and adventure that children have, while still retaining our signature modern style. With clothes that children could easily wear while exploring and playing, through to more refined items that would be as comfortable in a festive setting. Making the most of our core dark colours and tapping into our beautiful pastel shades also, there is something for everyone in this pattern book.

As before we have been guided by the MillaMia ethos that you should be able to combine a love of knitting with a love of modern contemporary design and quality. The designs in this book are clearly influenced by current trends, yet retain a timeless, classic appeal that we believe will transform the finished knitted item into heirlooms that people will want to keep. As ever our love of the Scandinavian design aesthetic has influenced everything from the designs to colour choices.

EXPLORING OUR COLOUR PALETTE

With this collection our goal was to try a few different combinations and as such you can find far more patterns that take advantage of the richness and depth of our dark shades – Midnight (101), Storm (102), Moss (103) and Claret (104) – frequently teaming them with one of our great neutral or light colours such as Fawn (160), Snow (124) and Forget me not (120). Some of the more delicate designs also make great use of our softer light shades, for instance Lilac Blossom (123) and Putty Grey (121), often brought to life with our now signature flash of contrast colour.

Lilian Jacket
in Lilac Blossom (123)
and Storm (102)
pattern on page 104

When we defined the MillaMia Naturally Soft Merino colours we worked really hard to arrive at a set of shades that we felt would work well together, complementing and enhancing each other. As such don't be scared of experimenting with different colour combinations yourself. While we present options and alternative colour suggestions, why not try personalising your knitting by selecting your own variation of these? If you look at our website, www.millamia.com, you will find a 'Colour Tool' that allows you to experiment, 'playing' with different combinations and making your own colour design decisions.

CREATING FUTURE HEIRLOOMS

Given how readily available cheap children's clothes are today, it is not really possible to view a hand knitted garment as an alternative to this. Rather we think a hand knit's value comes not just from the utility it offers as a layer of clothing. Instead it has an unquantifiable value from being lovingly hand-made, knitted with a special recipient in mind. It tells a story in its own right, and above all offers the creator the chance to enjoy a hobby they love.

To make the process of creating these treasured items as enjoyable as possible we felt it was important to offer our customers a high quality product. This means that from the strength of our designs, through to the presentation of our patterns and the standard of our yarn, high quality is a governing concept. Our Naturally Soft Merino yarn contains no acrylic and produces a lovely and soft item to wear. It is also a forgiving yarn that rewards experienced knitters with beautiful, springy cables and defined colourwork, while helping beginner knitters to achieve an even stitch definition. And not forgetting – machine washable.

WHERE CAN I LEARN MORE?

We hope to make knitting easy for you. So whether it is a new technique you are struggling with or if you are a complete novice there are some marvellous resources available to you. The internet is a wonderful thing – so many links and videos and tutorials at your fingertips just a search away. If you need a starting point log on to our website www.millamia.com and search through the 'Making Knitting Easy' section. There you can get advice, or download tools, email us a question for our technical experts, organise a knitting class or find someone who can help knit the item for you. Not forgetting to look locally too. You should seek out any yarn shops or haberdashery departments. Many of these are staffed with real experts who will be able to help you. A full list of MillaMia stockists is available from our website www.millamia.com – in these stores you will find people who are familiar and experienced with both the MillaMia yarns and patterns.

CONFUSED WITH A PATTERN?

We check every MillaMia pattern numerous times before we go to print. Despite this occasionally there can be errors in knitting patterns. If you see what you think is an error the best thing is to visit www.millamia.com where any errors that have been spotted will be published under 'Pattern Revisions'. If you cannot find the answer you are looking for, then do send an email (info@millamia.com) or contact us via the website and we will get back to you.

BASIC INFORMATION

SKILL LEVELS

Recognising that we are not all expert knitters we have graded each pattern in the book to allow you to gauge whether it is one that you feel confident to try. The grades are as follows:

Beginner: You have just picked up (or refound) knitting needles and are comfortable with the basic concepts of knitting. By reading carefully you can follow a pattern. Items such as scarves and blankets and simple jumpers are ideal for you to start with.

Beginner / Improving: Having knitted a few pieces you are now looking to try new things, for instance colour combinations and features such as pockets. You might surprise yourself by trying one of the simpler colourwork or cable patterns in this book – you will find that they are not as difficult as you may have thought. Bear in mind that most experienced knitters will be happy to help a beginner. Or look at our website for advice and help.

Improving: You have knitted a variety of items such as jumpers, cardigans and accessories in the past, and are comfortable with following patterns. You may have tried your hand at cable knitting and some form of colourwork before.

Experienced: You are comfortable with most knitting techniques. You have preferences and likes and dislikes, although are willing to try something new. You can read patterns quickly and are able to adapt them to your own requirements – for instance if resizing is needed.

YARN – SOME ADVICE

As there can be colour variations between dye lots when yarn is produced, we suggest that you buy all the yarn required for a project at the same time (with the same dye lot number) to ensure consistency of colour. The amount of yarn required for each pattern is based on average requirements meaning they are an approximate guide.

The designs in this book have been created specifically with a certain yarn composition in mind. The weight, quality, colours, comfort and finished knit effect of this yarn is ideally suited to these patterns. Substituting for another yarn may produce a garment that is different from the design and images in this book.

For some of the heavier items in this book we have used a technique where we 'use the yarn double'. This simply means using two balls of yarn at once on a thicker needle (in our patterns a 5mm (US 8) needle) to produce a thicker quality to the knitted fabric. An advantage of this technique is that the garment will be quicker to knit up.

TENSION / GAUGE

A standard tension is given for all the patterns in this book. As the patterns are in different stitch types (e.g. stocking, garter, rib, etc.) this tension may vary between patterns, and so you must check your tension against the recommendation at the start of the pattern. As matching the tension affects the final shape and size of the item you are knitting it can have a significant impact if it is not matched. Ensuring that you are knitting to the correct tension will result in the beautiful shape and lines of the original designs being achieved.

To check your tension we suggest that you knit a square according to the tension note at the start of each pattern (casting on an additional 10 or more stitches to the figure given in the tension note and knitting 5 to 10 more rows than specified in the tension note). You should knit the tension square in the stitch given in the note (e.g. stocking, garter, moss, etc). Once knitted, mark out a 10cm by 10cm / 4in by 4in square using pins and count the number of stitches and rows contained within. If your tension does not quite match the one given try switching to either finer needles (if you have too few stitches in your square) or thicker needles (if you have too many stitches) until you reach the desired tension.

USEFUL RESOURCES

We believe that using quality trims with our knitwear gives the garments a professional finishing touch. Visit your local yarn/ haberdashery shop for these items and MillaMia yarn or visit www.millamia.com to order yarn directly or find local stockists.

SIZES

Alongside the patterns in this book we give measurements for the items – as two children of the same age can have very different measurements, this should be used as a guide when choosing which size to knit. The best way to ensure a good fit is to compare the actual garment measurements given in the pattern with the measurements of an existing garment that fits the child well.

Please note that where a chest measurement is given in the table at the top of each pattern this refers to the total measurement of the garment around the chest. When the cross chest measurement is given graphically in the accompanying diagrams this is half the around chest measurement. Children's clothes are designed with plenty of 'ease', this means that there is not as much shaping or fit to a child's garment as you will find in adult knitwear.

CARE OF YOUR GARMENT

See the ball band of MillaMia Naturally Soft Merino for washing and pressing instructions. Make sure you reshape your garments while they are wet after washing, and dry flat.

LANGUAGE

This book has been written in UK English. However, where possible US terminology has also been included and we have provided a translation of the most common knitting terms that differ between US and UK knitting conventions on page 9. In addition all sizes and measurements are given in both centimetres and inches throughout. Remember that when a knitting pattern refers to the left and right sides of an item it is referring to the left or right side as worn, rather than as you are looking at it.

READING COLOUR CHARTS

For some of the patterns in this book there are colour charts included. In a colour chart one square represents one stitch and one row. A key shows what each colour in the chart refers to.

The bottom row of the chart indicates the first row of knitting, and as you work your way up, each row of the chart illustrates the next row of knitting. Repeats are the same for all sizes, however different sizes will often require extra stitches as the repeat will not exactly fit. These stitches are marked by vertical lines showing the start and end of rows.

Additional specific instructions are given regarding how to read each chart in the 'Note' at the start of each pattern.

Filip Tank Top in Midnight (101), Forget me not (120), Snow (124), Grass (141), Scarlet (140), Seaside (161), Moss (103), Storm (102), Claret (104), and Lilac Blossom (123) pattern on page 72

Alexander Jacket in Midnight (101)
and Fawn (160)
pattern on page 28

8

ABBREVIATIONS

alt	alternate
approx	approximately
beg	begin(ning)
cont	continue
dec	decrease(ing)
foll	following
g-st	garter stitch
inc	increase(ing)
k or K	knit
k2 tog	knit two stitches together
m1	make one stitch by picking up the loop lying before the next stitch and knitting into back of it
m1p	make one stitch by picking up the loop lying before the next stitch and purling into back of it
mths	months
p or P	purl
p2 tog	purl two stitches together
patt	pattern
psso	pass slipped stitch over
pwise	purlwise
rib2 tog	rib two stitches together according to rib pattern being followed
rem	remain(ing)
rep	repeat(ing)
skpo	slip one, knit one, pass slipped stitch over – one stitch decreased
sl	slip stitch
st(s)	stitch(es)
st st	stocking stitch
tbl	through back of loop
tog	together
yf	yarn forward
yo	yarn over
yon	yarn over needle to make a st
yrn	yarn round needle
y2rn	wrap the yarn two times around needle. On the following row work into each loop separately working tbl into second loop
[]	work instructions within brackets as many times as directed

UK AND US KNITTING TRANSLATIONS

UK	US
Cast off	Bind off
Colour	Color
Grey	Gray
Join	Sew
Moss stitch	Seed stitch
Tension	Gauge
Stocking stitch	Stockinette stitch
Yarn forward	Yarn over
Yarn over needle	Yarn over
Yarn round needle	Yarn over
y2rn	yo2

KNITTING NEEDLE CONVERSION CHART

Metric, mm	US size
2	0
2.25	1
2.5	1
2.75	2
3	2
3.25	3
3.5	4
3.75	5
4	6
4.25	6
4.5	7
5	8
5.5	9
6	10
6.5	10.5
7	10.5
7.5	11
8	11
9	13
10	15

From left to right: **Charlotte Cardigan** in Putty Grey (121) pattern on page 12, **Karin Shrug** in Putty Grey (121) pattern on page 24 and **Lova Babygrow** in Putty Grey (121) and Petal (122) pattern on page 18

CHARLOTTE
CARDIGAN
LOVA
BABYGROW
KARIN
SHRUG

CHARLOTTE CARDIGAN

SKILL LEVEL **Improving**

SIZES / MEASUREMENTS

To fit age	2-3	3-4	4-5	5-6	6-7	years

ACTUAL GARMENT MEASUREMENTS

Chest	60	65	70	75	80	cm
	23 ½	25 ½	27 ½	29 ½	31 ½	in
Length to shoulder	40	43	46	49	52	cm
	15 ¾	17	18	19 ¼	20 ½	in
Sleeve length	22	25	28	31	33	cm
	8 ¾	9 ¾	11	12 ¼	13	in

MATERIALS

7(8:9:9:10) 50g/1 ¾oz balls of MillaMia Naturally Soft Merino in Putty Grey (121).
Pair each of 2.75mm (US 2) and 3.25mm (US 3) knitting needles.
Cable needle.
One large (approx 18mm/¾in diameter) and one small (approx 15mm/½in diameter) button.

TENSION / GAUGE

25 sts and 34 rows to 10cm/4in square over st st using 3.25mm (US 3) needles.

HINTS AND TIPS

Super stylish and versatile – this cardigan is a sure fire winner. Loved by the knitter for the cable panels and by modern mums for its stylish design. Pay attention early on in the pattern to make sure you get the panels and garter stitch borders on the front pieces set correctly and then enjoy the knitting on this super item!

ABBREVIATIONS

C6B cable 6 back – slip next 3 sts onto cable needle and hold at back of work, k3, then k3 from cable needle.
C6F cable 6 front – slip next 3 sts onto cable needle and hold at front of work, k3, then k3 from cable needle.
See also page 9.

SUGGESTED ALTERNATIVE COLOURWAYS

Plum	Snow	Petal	Storm
162	124	122	102

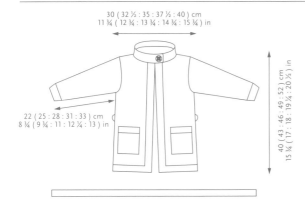

30 (32 ½ : 35 : 37 ½ : 40) cm
11 ¾ (12 ¾ : 13 ¾ : 14 ¾ : 15 ¾) in

22 (25 : 28 : 31 : 33) cm
8 ¾ (9 ¾ : 11 : 12 ¼ : 13) in

40 (43 : 46 : 49 : 52) cm
15 ¾ (17 : 18 : 19 ¼ : 20 ½) in

CABLE PANEL (worked over 19 sts)

1st row P2, k15, p2.
2nd and every foll wrong side row K2, p15, k2.
3rd row P2, k3, [C6F] twice, p2.
5th and 7th rows As 1st row.
9th row P2, [C6B] twice, k3, p2.
11th row As 1st row.
12th row As 2nd row.
These 12 rows form the cable panel and are repeated throughout.

BACK

With 2.75mm (US 2) needles cast on 108(114:120:126:132) sts.
K 9 rows.
Change to 3.25mm (US 3) needles.
Next row K16(18:20:22:24), p2, k3, [m1, k3] 3 times,
p2, k44(46:48:50:52), p2, k3, [m1, k3] 3 times, p2,
k16(18:20:22:24). 114(120:126:132:138) sts.
Next row P16(18:20:22:24), k2, p15, k2, p44(46:48:50:52), k2,
p15, k2, p16(18:20:22:24).
Work in patt as follows:
Next row K16(18:20:22:24), work across the 3rd row of cable
panel, k44(46:48:50:52), work across the 3rd row of cable
panel, k16(18:20:22:24).
Next row P16(18:20:22:24), work across the 4th row of cable
panel, p44(46:48:50:52), work across the 4th row of cable
panel, p16(18:20:22:24).
These 2 rows set the 12 row cable panel.
Work a further 4 rows.
Dec row K14(16:18:20:22), skpo, patt 19, k2 tog,
k40(42:44:46:48), skpo, patt 19, k2 tog, k14(16:18:20:22).
Work a further 9(9:11:11:13) rows.
Dec row K13(15:17:19:21), skpo, patt 19, k2 tog,
k38(40:42:44:46), skpo, patt 19, k2 tog, k13(15:17:19:21).
Work a further 9(9:11:11:13) rows.
Cont in this way dec 4 sts on next and 4 foll
10th(10th:12th:12th:14th) rows. 86(92:98:104:110) sts.

Work straight until back measures 27(29:31:33:35)cm/10 ¾(11 ½:
12 ¼:13:13 ¾)in from cast on edge, ending with a wrong side row.
Shape armholes
Cast off 5 sts at beg of next 2 rows. 76(82:88:94:100) sts.
Next row K2, skpo, patt to last 4 sts, k2 tog, k2.
Next row Patt to end.
Rep the last 2 rows 0(1:2:3:4) times more. 74(78:82:86:90) sts.
Cont in patt until back measures 40(43:46:49:52)cm/15 ¾(17:
18:19 ¼:20 ½)in from cast on edge, ending with a wrong side row.
Shape shoulders
Cast off 7 sts at beg of next 4 rows and 7(8:9:10:11) sts at beg
of foll 2 rows.
Leave rem 32(34:36:38:40) sts on a holder.

LEFT FRONT

With 2.75mm (US 2) needles cast on 57(60:63:66:69) sts.
K 9 rows.
Change to 3.25mm (US 3) needles.
Next row K16(18:20:22:24), p2, k3, [m1, k3] 3 times, p2,
k25(26:27:28:29). 60(63:66:69:72) sts.
Next row K8, p17(18:19:20:21), k2, p15, k2, p16(18:20:22:24).
Work in patt as follows:
Next row K16(18:20:22:24), work across the 3rd row of cable
panel, k25(26:27:28:29).
Next row K8, p17(18:19:20:21), work across the 4th row of
cable panel, p16(18:20:22:24).
These 2 rows set the 12 row cable panel and g-st front border.
Work a further 4 rows.
Dec row K14(16:18:20:22), skpo, patt 19, k2 tog, k23(24:25:26:27).
Work a further 9(9:11:11:13) rows.
Dec row K13(15:17:19:21), skpo, patt 19, k2 tog, k22(23:24:25:26).
Work a further 9(9:11:11:13) rows.
Cont in this way dec 2 sts on next and 4 foll
10th(10th:12th:12th:14th) rows. 46(49:52:55:58) sts.
Work straight until front measures 27(29:31:33:35)cm/10 ¾(11 ½:
12 ¼:13:13 ¾)in from cast on edge, ending with a wrong side row.

Shape armhole

Next row Cast off 5 sts, patt to end. 41(44:47:50:53) sts.

Next row Patt to end.

Next row K2, skpo, patt to end.

Next row Patt to end.

Rep the last 2 rows 0(1:2:3:4) times more. 40(42:44:46:48) sts.

Cont in patt until front measures 35(38:41:44:47)cm/13 ¾(15:16: 17 ¼:18 ½)in from cast on edge, ending with a wrong side row.

Shape front neck

Next row Patt to last 11(12:13:14:15) sts, turn and leave these sts on a holder.

Dec one st at neck edge on next 8 rows.

Work straight until front measures the same as back to shoulder, ending at armhole edge.

Shape shoulder

Cast off 7 sts at beg of next and foll right side row.

Work 1 row.

Cast off rem 7(8:9:10:11) sts.

RIGHT FRONT

With 2.75mm (US 2) needles cast on 57(60:63:66:69) sts.

K 9 rows.

Change to 3.25mm (US 3) needles.

Next row K25(26:27:28:29), p2, k3, [m1, k3] 3 times, p2, k16(18:20:22:24). 60(63:66:69:72) sts.

Next row P16(18:20:22:24), k2, p15, k2, p17(18:19:20:21), k8.

Work in patt as follows:

Next row K25(26:27:28:29), work across the 3rd row of cable panel, k16(18:20:22:24).

Next row P16(18:20:22:24), work across the 4th row of cable panel, p17(18:19:20:21), k8.

These 2 rows set the 12 row cable panel and g-st front border.

Work a further 4 rows.

Dec row K23(24:25:26:27), skpo, patt 19, k2 tog, k14(16:18:20:22).

Work a further 9(9:11:11:13) rows.

Dec row K22(23:24:25:26), skpo, patt 19, k2 tog, k13(15:17:19:21).

Work a further 9(9:11:11:13) rows.

Cont in this way dec 2 sts on next and 4 foll 10th(10th:12th:12th:14th) rows. 46(49:52:55:58) sts.

Work straight until front measures 27(29:31:33:35)cm/10 ¾(11 ½: 12 ¼:13:13 ¾)in from cast on edge, ending with a right side row.

Shape armhole

Next row Cast off 5 sts, patt to end. 41(44:47:50:53) sts.

Next row Patt to last 4 sts, k2 tog, k2.

Next row Patt to end.

Rep the last 2 rows 0(1:2:3:4) times more. 40(42:44:46:48) sts.

Cont in patt until front measures 35(38:41:44:47)cm/13 ¾(15:16: 17 ¼:18 ½)in from cast on edge, ending with a wrong side row.

Shape front neck

Next row Patt 11(12:13:14:15) sts, leave these sts on a holder, patt to end.

Dec one st at neck edge on next 8 rows.

Work straight until front measures the same as back to shoulder, ending at armhole edge.

Shape shoulder

Cast off 7 sts at beg of next and foll wrong side row.

Work 1 row.

Cast off rem 7(8:9:10:11) sts.

SLEEVES

With 2.75mm (US 2) needles cast on 49(49:59:59:69) sts.

1st row (right side) P3, [k3, p2] to last 6 sts, k3, p3.

2nd row K3, [p3, k2] to last 6 sts, p3, k3.

Rep the last 2 rows 5 times more, and then the 1st row again.

Inc row (wrong side) Rib 21(21:26:26:31) m1, rib 7, m1, rib 21(21:26:26:31). 51(51:61:61:71) sts.

Change to 3.25mm (US 3) needles.

Work in patt as follows:

1st row K16(16:21:21:26), work across 3rd row of cable panel, k16(16:21:21:26).

2nd row P16(16:21:21:26), work across 4th row of patt panel, k16(16:21:21:26).

These 2 rows set the cable panel.

Work a further 8 rows.

Inc row K3, m1, patt to last 3 sts, m1, k3.

Work 5(3:5:3:5) rows.

Rep the last 6(4:6:4:6) rows 6(10:7:11:8) times more, and then the inc row again. 67(75:79:87:91) sts.

Cont straight until sleeve measures 22(25:28:31:33)cm/8 ¾(9 ¾: 11:12 ¼:13)in from cast on edge, ending with a wrong side row.

Shape sleeve top

Cast off 5 sts at beg of next 2 rows. 57(65:69:77:81) sts.

Next row K2, skpo, patt to last 4 sts, k2 tog, k2.

Next row Patt to end.

Rep the last 2 rows 0(1:2:3:4) times more. 55(61:63:69:71) sts.

Cast off 2 sts at beg of next 20(22:24:26:28) rows.

Cast off.

NECKBAND

Join shoulder seams.

With right side facing and 2.75mm (US 2) needles slip 11(12:13:14:15) sts from right front neck holder onto a needle, pick up and k20 sts up right front neck, k32(34:36:38:40) sts from back neck holder, pick up and k20 sts down left front neck, k11(12:13:14:15) from left front holder. 94(98:102:106:110) sts.

Cast on 5 sts at beg of next 2 rows. 104(108:112:116:120) sts.

K 5 rows.

Next row (buttonhole row) K3, k2 tog, y2rn, skpo, k to last 6 sts, k2 tog, yf, k4.

K 7 rows.

Cast off.

POCKETS (make 2)

With 3.25mm (US 3) needles cast on 24(26:28:30:32) sts.

1st row K4(5:6:7:8), p2, k12, p2, k4(5:6:7:8).

2nd row P4(5:6:7:8), k2, p12, k2, p4(5:6:7:8).

3rd row K4(5:6:7:8), p2, k3, [m1, k3] 3 times, p2, k4(5:6:7:8). 27(29:31:33:35) sts.

4th row P4(5:6:7:8), k2, p15, k2, p4(5:6:7:8).

Work in patt as follows:

Next row K4(5:6:7:8), work across the 3rd row of cable panel, k4(5:6:7:8).

Next row P4(5:6:7:8), work across the 4th row of cable panel, p4(5:6:7:8).

These 2 rows set the 12 row cable panel.

Work a further 33 rows.

Next row P4(5:6:7:8), k2, [p2 tog, p1] 5 times, k2, p4(5:6:7:8). 22(24:26:28:30) sts.

Change to 2.75mm (US 2) needles.

K 10 rows.

Cast off.

BELT

Using 2.75mm (US 2) needles, cast on 10 sts.

Cont in g-st until belt measures 90(95:100:105:110)cm/ 35 ½(37 ½:39 ½:41 ¼:43 ¼)in.

Cast off.

BELT CARRIERS (make 2)

Using 2.75mm (US 2) needles, cast on 12 sts.

K 1 row.

Cast off.

MAKE UP

Join side and sleeve seams. Sew in sleeves. Sew on pockets. Sew belt carriers to side seam. Sew on buttons.

LOVA BABYGROW

SKILL LEVEL **Experienced**

SIZES / MEASUREMENTS

To fit age	0-3	3-6	6-12	mths

ACTUAL GARMENT MEASUREMENTS

Chest	53	57	60	cm
	21	22 ½	23 ½	in
Length to	44	48	53	cm
shoulder	17 ¼	19	21	in
Sleeve	14	16	18	cm
length	5 ½	6 ¼	7	in
Inside leg	12	14	17	cm
length	4 ¾	5 ½	6 ¾	in

MATERIALS

3 (4:4) 50g/1 ¾oz balls of MillaMia Naturally Soft Merino in Petal (122) (M).
3 (3:4) balls of Putty Grey (121) (A).
Pair each of 2.75mm (US 2) and 3.25mm (US 3) knitting needles.
12 buttons (approx 14mm/½in diameter).

TENSION / GAUGE

25 sts and 34 rows to 10cm/4in square over st st using 3.25mm (US 3) needles.

HINTS AND TIPS

This is a wonderful gift for any newborn baby. The beautiful stripes in this design result in quite a number of loose ends to darn in. To avoid having to do them all at once at the end of the project, why not try to sew them in every now and again along the way?

ABBREVIATIONS

See page 9.

SUGGESTED ALTERNATIVE COLOURWAYS

| Forget me not 120 | Putty Grey 121 | Snow 124 | Fawn 160 | Daisy Yellow 142 | Fuchsia 143 | Seaside 161 | Scarlet 140 |

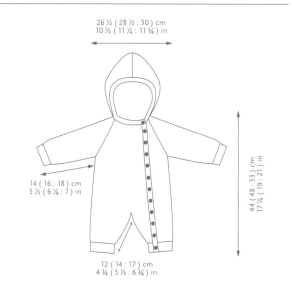

26 ½ (28 ½ : 30) cm
10 ½ (11 ¼ : 11 ¾) in

14 (16 : 18) cm
5 ½ (6 ¼ : 7) in

44 (48 : 53) cm
17 ¼ (19 : 21) in

12 (14 : 17) cm
4 ¾ (5 ½ : 6 ¾) in

BACK

First leg

With 2.75mm (US 2) needles and M, cast on 22(24:26) sts.

Rib row [K1, p1] to end.

Rep the last row for 2(3:4)cm/¾(1¼:1½)in, ending with a right side row.

Inc row Rib 3(2:1), [m1, rib 4] 4(5:6) times, m1, rib 3(2:1). 27(30:33) sts.

Join on A.

Change to 3.25mm (US 3) needles.

Cont in st st and stripes of 3 rows A and 3 rows M.

Work 0(2:6) rows.

Inc row K4, m1, k to end.

P 1 row.

Rep the last 2 rows 14 times more, and then the inc row again. 43(46:49) sts.

Cont straight until leg measures 12(14:17)cm/4¾(5½:6¾)in ending with a p row.

Shape crotch

Next row Cast off 4 sts, k to end. 39(42:45) sts.

P 1 row.

Leave these sts on a holder.

Second leg

With 2.75mm (US 2) needles and M, cast on 22(24:26) sts.

Rib row [K1, p1] to end.

Rep the last row for 2(3:4)cm/ ¾(1¼:1½)in, ending with a right side row.

Inc row Rib 3(2:1), [m1, rib 4] 4(5:6) times, m1, rib 3(2:1). 27(30:33) sts.

Join on A.

Change to 3.25mm (US 3) needles.

Cont in st st and stripes of 3 rows A and 3 rows M.

Work 0(2:6) rows.

Inc row K to last 4 sts, m1, k4.

P 1 row.

Rep the last 2 rows 14 times more, and then the inc row again. 43(46:49) sts.

Cont straight until leg measures 12(14:17)cm/4¾(5½:6¾)in ending with a k row.

Shape crotch

Next row Cast off 4 sts, p to end. 39(42:45) sts.

Next row K38(41:44), k last st tog with first st on first leg, k38(41:44). 77(83:89) sts.

Next row P to end.

Next row K34(36:38), skpo, k5(7:9), k2 tog, k34(36:38).

Next row P to end.

Next row K34(36:38), skpo, k3(5:7), k2 tog, k34(36:38).

Next row P to end.

Next row K34(36:38), skpo, k1(3:5), k2 tog, k34(36:38).

2nd and 3rd sizes only

Next row P to end.

Next row K-(36:38), skpo, k-(1:3), k2 tog, k-(36:38).

3rd size only

Next row P to end.

Next row K-(-:38), skpo, k-(-:1), k2 tog, k-(-:38).

All sizes

Next row P to end.

Next row K34(36:38), s1 1, k2 tog, psso, k34(36:38). 69(73:77) sts.

Cont straight until back measures 32(35:38)cm/ 12½(13¾:15)in from cast on edges, ending with a p row.

Shape armholes

Cast off 4 sts at beg of next 2 rows. 61(65:69) sts.

Next row K4, skpo, k to last 6 sts, k2 tog, k4.

Next row P to end.

Rep the last 2 rows 18(19:20) times more. 23(25:27) sts.

Cast off.

LEFT FRONT

With 2.75mm (US 2) needles and M, cast on 14(16:16) sts.
Rib row [K1, p1] to end.
Rep the last row for 2(3:4)cm/¾(1 ¼:1 ½)in, ending with a right side row.
Inc row Rib 1(1:1), [m1, rib 2(3:2)] 6(5:6) times, m1, rib 1(0:3). 21(22:23) sts.
Join on A.
Change to 3.25mm (US 3) needles.
Cont in st st and stripes of 3 rows A and 3 rows M.
Work straight until front measures the same as back to armhole, ending at armhole edge.
Shape armhole
Next row Cast off 4 sts, k to end. 17(18:19) sts.
Next row P to end.
Next row K1, skpo, k to end.
Rep the last 2 rows until 2 sts rem, ending with a p row.
Cast off.

RIGHT FRONT

First leg
With 2.75mm (US 2) needles and M, cast on 22(24:26) sts.
Rib row [K1, p1] to end.
Rep the last row for 2(3:4)cm/¾(1 ¼:1 ½)in, ending with a right side row.
Inc row Rib 3(2:1), [m1, rib 4] 4(5:6) times, m1, rib 3(2:1). 27(30:33) sts.
Join on A.
Change to 3.25mm (US 3) needles.
Cont in st st and stripes of 3 rows A and 3 rows M.
Work 0(2:6) rows.
Inc row K4, m1, k to end.
P 1 row.
Rep the last 2 rows 14 times more, and then the inc row again. 43(46:49) sts.
Cont straight until leg measures 12(14:17)cm/4 ¾(5 ½:6 ¾)in ending with a p row.
Shape crotch
Next row Cast off 4 sts, k to end. 39(42:45) sts.
P 1 row.
Leave these sts on a holder.
Second leg
With 2.75mm (US 2) needles and M, cast on 4(6:8) sts.
Rib row [K1, p1] to end.
Rep the last row for 2(3:4)cm/¾(1 ¼:1 ½)in, ending with a right side row.
Inc row Rib 2(3:4), m1, rib 2(3:4). 5(7:9) sts.
Join on A.
Change to 3.25mm (US 3) needles.
Cont in st st and stripes of 3 rows A and 3 rows M.
Work 0(2:6) rows.
Inc row K to last 4 sts, m1, k4.
P 1 row.
Rep the last 2 rows 14 times more, and then the inc row again. 21(23:25) sts.

Cont straight until leg measures 12(14:17)cm/4 ¾(5 ½:6 ¾)in ending with a k row.

Shape crotch

Next row Cast off 4 sts, p to end. 17(19:21) sts.

Next row K16(18:20), k last st tog with first st on first leg, k38(41:44). 55(60:65) sts.

Next row P to end.

Next row K12(13:14), skpo, k5(7:9), k2 tog, k34(36:38).

Next row P to end.

Next row K12(13:14), skpo, k3(5:7), k2 tog, k34(36:38).

Next row P to end.

Next row K12(13:14), skpo, k1(3:5), k2 tog, k34(36:38).

2nd and 3rd sizes only

Next row P to end.

Next row K-(13:14), skpo, k-(1:3), k2 tog, k-(36:38).

3rd size only

Next row P to end.

Next row K-(-:14), skpo, k-(-:1), k2 tog, k. -(-:38).

All sizes

Next row P to end.

Next row K12(13:14), s1 1, k2 tog, psso, k34(36:38). 47(50:53) sts.

Cont straight until front measures same as back to armhole, ending at armhole edge.

Shape armhole

Next row Cast off 4 sts, p to end. 43(46:49) sts.

Next row K to last 3 sts, k2 tog, k1.

Next row P to end.

Rep the last 2 rows 14(15:16) times more. 28(30:32) sts.

Cast off.

LEFT SLEEVE

With 2.75mm (US 2) needles and M cast on 34(36:38) sts.

Rib row [K1, p1] to end.

Rep the last row for 2(3:4)cm/¾(1 ¼:1 ½)in, ending with a wrong side row, inc one st at centre of last row. 35(37:39) sts. Join on A.

Change to 3.25mm (US 3) needles.

Cont in st st and stripes of 3 rows A and 3 rows M.

Work 2 rows.

Inc row K3, m1, k to last 3 sts, m1, k3.

Work 5(5:3) rows.

Rep the last 6(6:4) rows 4(5:7) times more, and then the inc row again. 47(51:57) sts.

Cont straight until sleeve measures approx 14(16:18)cm/ 5 ½(6 ¼:7)in from cast on edge, ending with the same colour stripe as on back before armhole shaping.

Shape sleeve top

Cast off 4 sts at beg of next 2 rows. 39(43:49) sts.

Next row K4, skpo, k to last 6 sts, k2 tog, k4.

Next row P to end.

Next row K to end.

Next row P to end.

Rep the last 4 rows 3(3:2) times more. 31(35:43) sts.

Next row K4, skpo, k to last 6 sts, k2 tog, k4.

Next row P to end.

Rep the last 2 rows until 17(19:21) sts rem, ending with a p row ***.

Shape top

Next row K4, skpo, k to end.

Next row Cast off 2 sts, p to end.

Rep the last 2 rows 3 times more. 5(7:9) sts.

Cast off.

RIGHT SLEEVE

Work as given for left sleeve to ***.
Shape top
Next row Cast off 2 sts, k to last 6 sts, k2 tog, k4.
Next row P to end.
Rep the last 2 rows 3 times more. 5(7:9) sts.
Cast off.

HOOD

Join raglan seams.
Using 3.25mm (US 3) needles and M, pick up and k20(22:24) sts
across top of right sleeve, 23(25:27) sts across back neck,
20(22:24) sts across top of left sleeve. 63(69:75) sts.
Beg with a p row cont in st st and rows of 2 rows M, then
[3 rows A and 3 rows M] to end.
Work straight until hood measures 18(19:20)cm/7(7 ½:8)in,
ending with a p row.
Shape top
Next row K 31(34:37), turn and work on these sts.
Cast off 5 sts at beg of next and 3 foll wrong side rows.
Next row K to end.
Next row Cast off 5(6:7) sts, p to end.
Next row K to end.
Cast off rem 6(8:10) sts.
With right side facing rejoin yarn to rem sts, cast off one st,
k to end.
Next row P to end.
Cast off 5 sts at beg of next and 3 foll right side rows.
Next row P to end.
Next row Cast off 5(6:7) sts, k to end.
Next row P to end.
Cast off rem 6(8:10) sts.

Edging
Join top seam.
With right side facing, using 2.75mm (US 2) needles and M
pick up and k28(30:32) sts across front neck, pick up and
k121(127:133) sts around row ends of hood.
1st row K1, [p1, k1] to end.
2nd row P1, [k1, p1] to end.
Rep the last 2 rows twice, and then the 1st row again.
Cast off in rib.

BUTTON BAND

With right side facing, using 2.75mm (US 2) needles and M
pick up and k 111(121:131) sts evenly along left front edge.
1st rib row P1, [k1, p1] to end.
2nd rib row K1, [p1, k1] to end.
Rep the last 2 rows once more, and then the 1st row again.
Cast off in rib.

BUTTONHOLE BAND

With right side facing, using 2.75mm (US 2) needles and M
pick up and k111(121:133) sts evenly along right front edge.
1st rib row P1, [k1, p1] to end.
2nd rib row K1, [p1, k1] to end.
Buttonhole row Rib 5(5:5), yrn, rib 2 tog, [rib 7(8:9), yrn, rib 2
tog] 11 times, rib 5(4:5).
Rib 2 more rows.
Cast off in rib.

MAKE UP

Join side and sleeve seams. Join under arm seams. Sew on
buttons. Join inner legs.

KARIN SHRUG

SKILL LEVEL **Beginner / Improving**

SIZES / MEASUREMENTS

To fit age	1-2	2-3	3-4	4-5	years

ACTUAL GARMENT MEASUREMENTS

Length to shoulder	18 7	21 8 ¼	24 9 ½	27 10 ½	cm in
Sleeve length	5 2	5 2	5 2	5 2	cm in

MATERIALS

2(2:3:3) 50g/1 ¾oz balls of MillaMia Naturally Soft Merino in Plum (162).
Pair of 3.25mm (US 3) knitting needles.
Cable needle.

TENSION / GAUGE

25 sts and 34 rows to 10cm/4in square over st st using 3.25mm (US 3) needles.

HINTS AND TIPS

So simple – the main part is just one flat piece with a single cable running through it. Perfect for all seasons.

ABBREVIATIONS

C12F cable 12 front – slip next 6 sts on to a cable needle and hold at front of work, k6 then k6 from cable needle.
See also page 9.

SUGGESTED ALTERNATIVE COLOURWAYS

Putty Grey
121

Lilac Blossom
123

Fuchsia
143

Claret
104

MAIN PART

With 3.25mm (US 3) needles cast on 69(77:85:93) sts.
1st row (right side) [P1, k2] 4 times, p2, k12, p2, [k4, p4] 3(4:5:6) times, k4, p1, [k2, p1] 4 times.
2nd and every foll alt row P to end.
3rd and 5th rows As 1st row.
7th row [P1, k2] 4 times, p2, C12F, p2, [k4, p4] 3(4:5:6) times, k4, p1, [k2, p1] 4 times.
9th and 11th rows As 1st row.
12th row P to end.
These 12 rows form the patt and are repeated throughout.
Cont in patt until work measures 33(37:41:45)cm/13(14 ½: 16:17 ¾) in from cast on edge, ending with a 12th row.
Cast off.

CUFFS (make 2)

With 3.25mm (US 3) needles cast on 13 sts.
1st row P1, [k2, p1] 4 times.
2nd row P to end.
Rep these 2 rows for 15(18:22:24)cm/6(7:8 ¾:9 ½)in ending with a p row.
Cast off.

TO MAKE UP

Leaving 12 sts free at each end, sew cuffs to cast on and cast off edges of main part.
Join cast off and cast on edges to form sleeve and side seams.

5 cm
2 in

18 (21:24:27) cm
7 (8 ¼ :9 ½ : 10 ½) in

From left to right: **Alexander Jacket** in Midnight (101) and Fawn (160) pattern on page 28 and **Kiki Jumper** in Claret (104) pattern on page 34

ALEXANDER JACKET
KIKI JUMPER

ALEXANDER JACKET

SKILL LEVEL **Beginner / Improving**

SIZES / MEASUREMENTS

| To fit age | ½-1 | 1-2 | 2-3 | 3-4 | 4-5 | 5-6 | 7-8 | years |

ACTUAL GARMENT MEASUREMENTS

Chest	54	59	64	68	73	78	83	cm
	21 ¼	23 ¼	25 ¼	26 ¾	28 ¾	30 ½	36 ½	in
Length to	28	31	34	38	42	46	50	cm
shoulder	11	12 ¼	13 ¼	15	16 ½	18	19 ¾	in
Sleeve	17	19	22	24	28	32	36	cm
length	6 ¾	7 ½	8 ¾	9 ½	11	12 ¾	14 ¼	in

MATERIALS

4(5:5:6:7:8:9) 50g /1 ¾oz balls of MillaMia Naturally Soft Merino in Moss (103) (M).
One ball of contrast Fawn (160) (C).
Pair each of 3mm (US 2) and 3.25mm (US 3) knitting needles.
Six buttons (approx 18mm/¾in diameter).

TENSION / GAUGE

25 sts and 34 rows to 10cm/4in square over st st using 3.25mm (US 3) needles.

HINTS AND TIPS

Press the buttonhole tabs and patches before you sew them on. Take your time on this final detail of attaching patches and tabs, and make an effort to line up the shoulder patches at the same height, as this will make all the difference. We think this item looks great in these strong military colours but it could equally be knitted in lighter or brighter shades. Try in softer shades for girls.

ABBREVIATIONS

See page 9.

SUGGESTED ALTERNATIVE COLOURWAYS

| Midnight | Fawn | Claret | Fawn | Plum | Fawn |
| 101 | 160 | 104 | 160 | 162 | 160 |

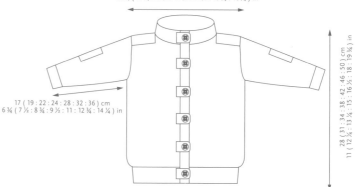

27 (29 ½ : 32 : 34 : 36 ½ : 39 : 41 ½) cm
10 ¾ (11 ¾ : 12 ½ : 13 ½ : 14 ½ : 15 ¼ : 16 ¼) in

17 (19 : 22 : 24 : 28 : 32) cm
6 ¾ (7 ½ : 8 ¾ : 9 ½ : 11 : 12 ¾ : 14 ¼) in

28 (31 : 34 : 38 : 42 : 46 : 50) cm
11 (12 ¼ : 13 ¼ : 15 : 16 ½ : 18 : 19 ¾) in

BACK

With 3mm (US 2) needles and M cast on
68(74:80:86:92:98:104) sts.
1st row K0(3:0:3:0:3:0), [p2, k4] to last 2(5:2:5:2:5:2) sts, p2,
k0(3:0:3:0:3:0).
2nd row P to end.
Rep the last 2 rows 8 times more.
Change to 3.25mm (US 3) needles.
Beg with a k row, work in st st until back measures
16(18:20:23:26:28:31)cm/6 ¼(7:8:9:10 ¼:11:12 ¼)in from cast
on edge, ending with a p row.
Shape armholes
Cast off 4 sts at beg of next 2 rows. 60(66:72:78:84:90:96) sts.
Next row K2, skpo, k to last 4 sts, k2 tog, k2.
Next row P to end.
Rep the last 2 rows 2(3:4:5:6:7:8) times.
54(58:62:66:70:74:78) sts.
Cont straight until back measures 28(31:34:38:42:46:50)cm/
11(12 ¼:13 ¼:15:16 ½:18:19 ¾)in from cast on edge, ending
with a p row.
Shape shoulders
Cast off 13(14:15:16:17:18:19) sts at beg of next 2 rows.
Leave rem 28(30:32:34:36:38:40) sts on a holder.

RIGHT FRONT

With 3mm (US 2) needles and M cast on
40(43:46:49:52:55:58) sts.
1st row P1, [k2, p1] 3 times, [k4, p2] 5(5:6:6:7:7:8) times,
k0(3:0:3:0:3:0).
2nd row P to end.
Rep the last 2 rows 8 times more.
Change to 3.25mm (US 3) needles.
Next row (right side) P1, [k2, p1] 3 times,
k30(33:36:39:42:45:48).
Next row P to end.
These 2 rows form the st st with rib border patt.
Work straight in patt until front measures
16(18:20:23:26:28:31)cm/6 ¼(7:8:9:10 ¼:11:12 ¼)in from cast
on edge, ending with a right side row.
Shape armhole
Cast off 4 sts at beg of next row. 36(39:42:45:48:51:54) sts.
Next row Patt to last 4 sts, k2 tog, k2.
Next row Patt to end.
Rep the last 2 rows 2(3:4:5:6:7:8) times.
33(35:37:39:41:43:45) sts.
Work straight until front measures 23(26:28:32:36:40:44)cm/
9(10 ¼:11:12 ½:14 ¼:15 ¾:17 ½)in from cast on edge, ending
with a wrong side row.
Shape neck
Next row Patt 13(14:15:16:17:18:19) sts, leave these sts on a
holder, k to end.
Next row P to end.
Next row K2, skpo, k to end.
Rep the last 2 rows until 13(14:15:16:17:18:19) sts rem.
Cont straight until front measures same as back to shoulder,
ending at armhole edge.
Shape shoulder
Cast off.
Mark positions for 5 of the buttons, the first 2 ½cm/1in from
cast on edge, the fifth 3cm/1 ¼in from neck edge and the rem
3 spaced evenly between.

LEFT FRONT

With 3mm (US 2) needles and M cast on
40(43:46:49:52:55:58) sts.
1st row K0(3:0:3:0:3:0), [p2, k4] 5(5:6:6:7:7:8) times, p1,
[k2, p1] 3 times.
2nd row P to end.
Rep the last 2 rows 3 times more.
Buttonhole row K0(3:0:3:0:3:0), [p2, k4] 5(5:6:6:7:7:8) times,
p1, k2, p2 tog, y2rn, skpo, k2, p1.
Work remaining buttonholes to match markers.
Next row P to end.
Work a further 8 rows.
Change to 3.25mm (US 3) needles.
Next row (right side) K30(33:36:39:42:45:48), p1, [k2, p1] 3 times.
Next row P to end.
These 2 rows form the st st with rib border patt.
Work straight in patt until front measures
16(18:20:23:26:28:31)cm/6 ¼(7:8:9:10 ¼:11:12 ¼)in from cast
on edge, ending with a wrong side row.
Shape armhole
Cast off 4 sts at beg of next row. 36(39:42:45:48:51:54) sts.
Next row Patt to end.
Next row K2, skpo, patt to end.
Rep the last 2 rows 2(3:4:5:6:7:8) times. 33(35:37:39:41:43:45) sts.
Work straight until front measures 23(26:28:32:36:40:44)cm/
9(10 ¼:11:12 ½:14 ¼:15 ¾:17 ½)in from cast on edge, ending
with a wrong side row.
Shape neck
Next row K to last 13(14:15:16:17:18:19) sts, leave these sts on
a holder.
Next row P to end.
Next row K to last 4 sts, k2 tog, k2.
Rep the last 2 rows until 13(14:15:16:17:18:19) sts rem.
Cont straight until front measures same as back to shoulder,
ending at armhole edge.
Shape shoulder
Cast off.

SLEEVES

With 3mm (US 2) needles and M cast on
32(32:38:44:44:50:56) sts.
1st row P2, [k4, p2] to end.
2nd row K2, [p4, k2] to end.
Rep the last 2 rows 6(6:7:7:8:8:8) times more.
Change to 3.25mm (US 3) needles.
Beg with a k row, work in st st.
Work 2 rows.
Inc row K3, m1, k to last 3 sts, m1, k3.
Work 5 rows.
Rep the last 6 rows 4(6:7:8:10:11:12) times more, and then the
inc row again. 44(48:56:64:68:76:84) sts.
Cont straight until sleeve measures 17(19:22:24:28:32:36)cm/
6 ¾(7 ½: 8 ¾:9 ½:11:12 ½ :14)in from cast on edge, ending
with a p row.
Shape sleeve top
Cast off 4 sts at beg of next 2 rows. 36(40:48:56:60:68:76) sts.
Next row K2, skpo, k to last 4 sts, k2 tog, k2.
Next row P to end.
Rep the last 2 rows 9(11:13:15:17:19:20) times.
16(16:20:24:24:28:34) sts.
Cast off 2 sts at beg of next 4(4:6:6:6:8:8) rows.
Cast off.

NECKBAND

Join shoulder seams.

With right side facing and 3mm (US 2) needles and M, slip 13(14:15:16:17:18:19) sts from right front neck holder onto a needle, pick up and k17(18:19:20:21:22:23) sts up right front neck, k28(30:32:34:36:38:40) sts from back neck holder, pick up and k17(18:19:20:21:22:23) sts down left front neck, patt 13(14:15:16:17:18:19) from left front holder. 88(94:100:106:112:118:124) sts.

Next row P to end.

Next row P1, [k2, p1] to end.

Rep the last 2 rows 3 times more.

Next row P to end.

Buttonhole row Patt to last 7 sts, k2 tog, y2rn, skpo, k2, p1.

Work a further 9(9:11:11:13:13:15) rows.

Cast off in patt.

BUTTONHOLE TABS (make 6)

With 3mm (US 2) needles and M cast on 10 sts.

1st row P1, [k2, p1] 3 times.

2nd row P to end.

Rep the last 2 rows once more.

Next row (buttonhole row) P1, k2, p2 tog, y2rn, skpo, k2, p1.

Work a further 15 rows in patt.

Cast off in patt.

ELBOW PATCHES (make 2)

With 3mm (US 2) needles and C cast on 16(19:19:22:22:25:25) sts.

1st row P1, [k2, p1] 5(6:6:7:7:8:8) times.

2nd row P to end.

Rep the last 2 rows 12(14:14:15:15:16:16) times more.

Cast off in patt.

SHOULDER PATCHES (make 2)

With 3mm (US 2) needles and C cast on 31(31:37:37:40:40:40) sts.

1st row P1, [k2, p1] 10(10:12:12:13:13:13) times.

2nd row P to end.

Rep the last 2 rows 8(9:10:10:11:11:12) times more.

Cast off in patt.

MAKE UP

Join side and sleeve seams. Sew in sleeves. Sew on button tabs and buttons.

Sew on shoulder and elbow patches.

KIKI JUMPER

SKILL LEVEL **Experienced**

SIZES / MEASUREMENTS

To fit age	1-2	3-4	5-6	7-8	years

ACTUAL GARMENT MEASUREMENTS

Chest	63	67	71	76	cm
	24 ¾	26 ½	28	30	in
Length to	39	44	49	54	cm
shoulder	15 ¼	17 ¼	19 ¼	21 ¼	in
Sleeve length	22	25	28	31	cm
with cuff folded back	8 ½	9 ¾	11	12	in

MATERIALS

6(7:8:9) 50g/1 ¾oz balls of MillaMia Naturally Soft Merino in Claret (104).
Pair each of 3mm (US 2) and 3.25mm (US 3) needles.
Cable needle.

TENSION / GAUGE

25 sts and 34 rows to 10cm/4in square over st st using 3.25mm (US 3) needles.

HINTS AND TIPS

A stunning cable pattern, take the time to study the picture so you can see how the cables will materialise. This will really reward perseverance and will look equally as impressive in a muted shade or a hot, bright colour. Block the rib on the collar and cuffs stretched and wide so that it is nice and comfortable.

ABBREVIATIONS

C4F cable 4 front – slip next 2 sts on to a cable needle and leave at front of work, k2, then k2 from cable needle.
C6F cable 6 front – slip next 3 sts on to a cable needle and leave at front of work, k3, then k3 from cable needle.
T4F twist 4 front – slip next 2 sts on to a cable needle and leave at front of work, p2, then k2 from cable needle.
T4B twist 4 back – slip next 2 sts on to a cable needle and leave at back of work, k2, then p2 from cable needle.
See also page 9.

SUGGESTED ALTERNATIVE COLOURWAYS

Midnight	Plum	Snow	Fawn
101	162	124	160

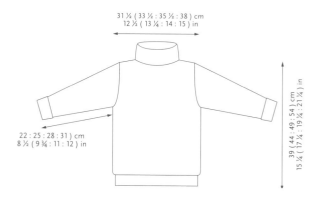

31 ½ (33 ½ : 35 ½ : 38) cm
12 ½ (13 ¼ : 14 : 15) in

39 (44 : 49 : 54) cm
15 ¼ (17 ¼ : 19 ¼ : 21 ¼) in

22 : 25 : 28 : 31) cm
8 ½ (9 ¾ : 11 : 12) in

CABLE PANEL A (worked over 6 sts)

1st row K6.
2nd row P6.
3rd row C6F.
4th row P6.
5th to 8th rows Rep 1st and 2nd rows twice.
9th row As 3rd row.
10th row P6.
11th to 20th rows Rep 1st and 2nd rows 5 times.
These 20 rows form the pattern and are repeated throughout.

PATT PANEL B (worked over 16 sts)

1st row P2, C4F, p4, C4F, p2.
2nd row K2, p4, k4, p4, k2.
3rd row P2, k4, p4, k4, p2.
4th row As 2nd row.
5th row As 1st row.
6th row As 2nd row.
7th row [T4B, T4F] twice.
8th row As 3rd row.
9th row K2, p4, C4F, p4, k2.
10th row As 3rd row.
11th row As 2nd row.
12th row As 3rd row
13th row As 9th row.
14th to 21st rows Rep the last 4 rows twice more.
22nd row As 3rd row.
23rd row [T4F, T4B] twice.
24th row As 2nd row.
These 24 rows form the pattern and are repeated throughout.

BACK

With 3mm (US 2) needles cast on 90(98:104:112) sts.
1st and 3rd sizes only
1st row P3, k4, p4, [k3, p4] 3 (-:4:-) times, [k2, p2] twice, k3, p4, k3, [p2, k2] twice, [p4, k3] 3 (-:4:-) times, p4, k4, p3.
2nd row K3, p4, k4, [p3, k4] 3 (-:4:-) times, [p2, k2] twice, p3, k4, p3, [k2, p2] twice, [k4, p3] 3 (-:4:-) times, k4, p4, k3.
3rd row P3, k4, p4, [k2, m1, k1, p4] 3 (-:4:-) times, [k2, p2] twice, k2, m1, k1, p4, k2, m1, k1, [p2, k2] twice, [p4, k2, m1, k1] 3 (-:4:-) times, p4, k4, p3. 98(-:114:-) sts.
4th row K3, [p4, k4] 4 (-:5:-) times, [p2, k2] twice, p4, k4, p4, [k2, p2] twice, [k4, p4] 4 (-:5:-) times, k3.
5th row P3, k4, p4, [C4F, p4] 3 (-:4:-) times, [k2, p2] twice, C4F, p4, C4F, [p2, k2] twice, [p4, C4F] 3 (-:4:-) times, p4, k4, p3.
6th row As 4th row.
7th row P3, [k4, p4] 4 (-:5:-) times, [k2, p2] twice, k4, p4, k4, [p2, k2] twice, [p4, k4] 4 (-:5:-) times, p3.
8th row As 4th row.
9th to 24th rows Rep 5th to 8th rows 4 times.
2nd and 4th sizes only
1st row K3, p4, k4, p4, [k3, p4] -(3:-:4) times, [k2, p2] twice, k3, p4, k3, [p2, k2] twice, [p4, k3] -(3:-:4) times, p4, k4, p4, k3.
2nd row P3, k4, p4, k4, [p3, k4] -(3:-:4) times, [p2, k2] twice, p3, k4, p3, [k2, p2] twice, [k4, p3] -(3:-:4) times, k4, p4, k4, p3.
3rd row K3, p4, k4, p4, [k2, m1, k1, p4] -(3:-:4) twice, k2, m1, k1, p4, k2, m1, k1, [p2, k2] twice, [p4, k2, m1, k1] -(3:-:4) times, p4, k4, p4, k3. -(106:-:122) sts.
4th row P3, k4, [p4, k4] -(4:-:5) times, [p2, k2] twice, p4, k4, p4, [k2, p2] twice, [k4, p4] -(4:-:5) times, k4, p3.
5th row K3, p4, k4, p4, [C4F, p4] -(3:-:4) times, [k2, p2] twice, C4F, p4, C4F, [p2, k2] twice, [p4, C4F] -(3:-:4) times, p4, k4, p4, k3.
6th row As 4th row.
7th row K3, p4, [k4, p4] -(4:-:5) times, [k2, p2] twice, k4, p4, k4, [p2, k2] twice, [p4, k4] -(4:-:5) times, p4, k3.
8th row As 4th row.
9th to 24th rows Rep 5th to 8th rows 4 times.

All sizes

Change to 3.25mm (US 3) needles.

1st row P11(15:11:15), [C4F, p4] 3(3:4:4) times, k2, p4, work across 1st row of patt panel B, p4, k2, [p4, C4F] 3(3:4:4) times, p11(15:11:15).

2nd row K11(15:11:15), [p4, k4] 3(3:4:4) times, p2, k4, work across 2nd row of patt panel B, k4, p2, [k4, p4] 3(3:4:4) times, k11(15:11:15).

3rd row P11(15:11:15), [k4, p4] 2(2:3:3) times, k1, m1, k2, m1, k1, p4, k2, p4, work across 3rd row of patt panel B, p4, k2, p4, k1, m1, k2, m1, k1, [p4, k4] 2(2:3:3) times, p11(15:11:15). 102(110:118:126) sts.

4th row K11(15:11:15), [p4, k4] 2(2:3:3) times, p6, k4, p2, k4, work across 4th row of patt panel B, k4, p2, k4, p6, [k4, p4] 2(2:3:3) times, k11(15:11:15).

5th row P11(15:11:15), [C4F, p4] 2(2:3:3) times, work across 7th row of patt panel A, p4, k2, p4, work across 5th row of patt panel B, p4, k2, p4, work across 7th row of patt panel A, [p4, C4F] 2(2:3:3) times, p11(15:11:15).

6th row K11(15:11:15), [p4, k4] 2(2:3:3) times, work across 8th row of patt panel A, k4, p2, k4, work across 6th row of patt panel B, k4, p2, k4, work across 8th row of patt panel A, [k4, p4] 2(2:3:3) times, k11(15:11:15).

7th row P11(15:11:15), [k4, p4] 2(2:3:3) times, work across 9th row of patt panel A, p4, k2, p4, work across 7th row of patt panel B, p4, k2, p4, work across 9th row of patt panel A, [p4, k4] 2(2:3:3) times, p11(15:11:15).

8th row K11(15:11:15), [p4, k4] 2(2:3:3) times, work across 10th row of patt panel A, k4, p2, k4, work across 8th row of patt panel B, k4, p2, k4, work across 10th row of patt panel A, [k4, p4] 2(2:3:3) times, k11(15:11:15).

These 8 rows form the 4 st cable panels and set the centre panel and 6 st cable panel.

Cont in patt until back measures 27(31:35:39)cm/10 ¾(12:13 ¾: 15 ¼)in from cast on edge, ending with a wrong side row.

Shape armholes

Cast off 4(5:6:7) sts at beg of next 2 rows. 94(100:106:112) sts.

Dec one st at each end of next 5(6:7:8) rows. 84(88:92:96) sts.

Keeping edge sts in reverse st st cont straight until back measures 37(42:47:52)cm/14 ½(16 ½:18 ½:20 ½)in from cast on edge, ending with a wrong side row.

Shape neck

Next row Patt 28(29:30:31), turn and work on these sts for first side of neck shaping.

Dec one st at neck edge on next 4 rows. 24(25:26:27) sts.

Work 1 row, ending at armhole edge.

Shape shoulder

Cast off.

With right side facing slip centre 28(30:32:34) sts on a holder, join on yarn, patt to end.

Complete to match first side.

FRONT

Work as given for back until front measures 35(39:43:47)cm/ 13 ¾(15 ¼:17:18 ½)in from cast on edge, ending with a wrong side row.

Shape neck

Next row Patt 33(34:35:36), turn and work on these sts for first side of neck shaping.

Dec one st at neck edge on next 9 rows. 24(25:26:27) sts.

Work straight until front matches back to shoulder shaping, ending at armhole edge.

Shape shoulder

Cast off.

With right side facing slip centre 18(20:22;24) sts on a holder, join on yarn, patt to end.

Complete to match first side.

SLEEVES

With 3.25mm (US 3) needles cast on 42(46:50:54) sts.
1st row K0(0:1:3), p1(3:4:4), k3, p4, [k2, p2] twice, k3, p4, k3, [p2, k2] twice, p4, k3, p1(3:4:4), k0(0:1:3).
2nd row P0(0:1:3), k1(3:4:4), p3, k4, [p2, k2] twice, p3, k4, p3, [k2, p2] twice, k4, p3, k1(3:4:4), p0(0:1:3).
These 2 rows form the rib.
Cont in rib until work measures 7cm/2 ¾in, ending with a 1st row.
Change to 3mm (US 2) needles.
Beg with a 1st row work a further 7cm/2 ¾in ending with a 2nd row.
Inc row K0(0:1:3), p1(3:4:4), k2, m1, k1, p4, [k2, p2] twice, k2, m1, k1, p4, k2, m1, k1, [p2, k2] twice, p4, k2, m1, k1, p1(3:4:4), k0(0:1:3). 46(50:54:58) sts.
Next row P0(0:1:3), k1(3:4:4), p4, k4, [p2, k2] twice, p4, k4, p4, [k2, p2] twice, k4, p4, k1(3:4:4), p0(0:1:3).
Change to 3.25mm (US 3) needles.
1st row P1(3:5:7), C4F, p4, k2, p4, work across 1st row of patt panel B, p4, k2, p4, C4F, p1(3:5:7).
2nd row K1(3:5:7), p4, k4, p2, k4, work across 2nd row of patt panel B, k4, p2, k4, p4, k1(3:5:7).
3rd row P1(3:5:7), k4, p4, k2, p4, work across 3rd row of patt panel B, p4, k2, p4, k4, p1(3:5:7).
4th row K1(3:5:7), p4, k4, p2, k4, work across 4th row of patt panel B, k4, p2, k4, p4, k1(3:5:7).
These 4 rows set the patt. Cont in patt as set, inc and work into reverse st st one st at each end of the next and every foll 4th(6th:6th:8th) row until there are 64(68:72:76) sts.
Cont straight until sleeve measures 29(32:35:38)cm/11 ½(12 ½: 13 ¾:15)in from cast on edge, ending with a wrong side row.
Shape sleeve top
Cast off 4(5:6:7) sts at beg of next 2 rows. 56(58:60:62) sts.
Dec one st at each end of next 3(4:5:6) rows. 50 sts.
Cast off 2 sts at beg of next 16 rows. 18 sts.
Cast off.

COLLAR

Join right shoulder seam.
With 3mm (US 2) needles and right side facing, pick up and k18(19:20:21) sts down left side of front neck, k across 18(20:22:24) sts at centre front from holder, pick up and k18(19:20:21) sts up right side of front neck, 8 sts down right side of back neck, k across 28(30:32:34) sts at back neck from holder, pick up and k8 sts up left side of back neck. 98(104:110:116) sts.
1st row P2, [k1, p2] to end.
2nd row K2, [p1, k2] to end.
Rep the last 2 rows 9(10:10:11) times more.
Change to 3.25mm (US 3) needles.
Inc row P2, [k1, m1, p2] to end.
Next row K2, [p2, k2] to end.
Cont in rib as set for a further 22(24:24:26) rows.
Cast off in rib.

MAKE UP

Join left shoulder seam and neckband, reversing seam to fold over. Sew on sleeves. Join side and sleeve seams, reversing seam to fold back.

From left to right: **Jonas Comfy Top** in Fawn (160) and Scarlet (140) pattern on page 50, **Nils Leggings** in Fawn (160) and Scarlet (140) pattern on page 46, **Nils Stripey Top** in Fawn (160) and Scarlet (140) pattern on page 42 and **Jonas Comfy Bottoms** in Fawn (160) and Scarlet (140) pattern on page 54

NILS
STRIPEY TOP
& LEGGINGS
# JONAS
COMFY TOP
& BOTTOMS

NILS STRIPEY TOP

SKILL LEVEL **Beginner / Improving**

SIZES / MEASUREMENTS

To fit age	0-3	3-6	6-12	12-18	18-24	24-36	36-48	mths

ACTUAL GARMENT MEASUREMENTS

Chest	51	54	58	60	64	67	70	cm
	20	21	23	23 ½	25	26 ½	27 ½	in
Length to	25	28	31	35	38	41	44	cm
shoulder	9 ¾	11	12 ¼	13 ¾	15	16 ¼	17 ½	in
Sleeve	15	17	19	21	23	25	27	cm
length	6	6 ¾	7 ½	8 ¼	9	9 ¾	10 ½	in

MATERIALS

2(2:2:2:3:3:4) 50g/1 ¾oz balls of MillaMia Naturally Soft Merino in each of Snow (124) (M) and Midnight (101) (C). Pair each of 3mm(US 2) and 3.25mm(US 3) knitting needles. 3 buttons (approx 18mm/¾in diameter).

TENSION / GAUGE

25 sts and 34 rows to 10cm/4in square over st st using 3.25mm (US 3) needles.

HINTS AND TIPS

We knew this top would be as popular for older children as it is for newborns so have tried to grade it in a wider range of sizes accordingly. This could easily be a girl's item too – just choose the colours to suit.

ABBREVIATIONS

See page 9.

SUGGESTED ALTERNATIVE COLOURWAYS

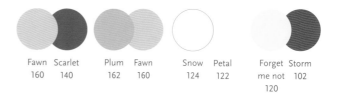

Fawn 160 Scarlet 140   Plum 162 Fawn 160   Snow 124 Petal 122   Forget me not 120 Storm 102

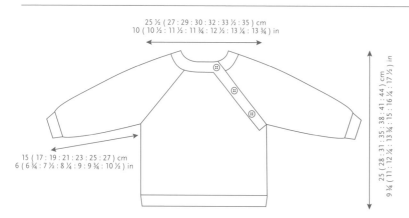

25 ½ (27 : 29 : 30 : 32 : 33 ½ : 35) cm
10 (10 ½ : 11 ½ : 11 ¾ : 12 ½ : 13 ¼ : 13 ¾) in

15 (17 : 19 : 21 : 23 : 25 : 27) cm
6 (6 ¾ : 7 ½ : 8 ¼ : 9 : 9 ¾ : 10 ½) in

25 (28 : 31 : 35 : 38 : 41 : 44) cm
9 ¾ (11 : 12 ¼ : 13 ¾ : 15 : 16 ¼ : 17 ½) in

BACK

With 3mm (US 2) needles and C, cast on
68(68:74:80:80:86:86) sts.
1st rib row K3, [p2, k4] to last 5 sts, p2, k3.
2nd rib row P3, [k2, p4] to last 5 sts, k2, p3.
These 2 rows form the rib.
Work a further 10(10:12:12:14:14:16) rows, dec(inc:-:
dec:inc:-:inc) 2(2:0:2:2:0:4) sts evenly across last row.
66(70:74:78:82:86:90) sts.
Cut off C.
Join on M.
Change to 3.25mm (US 3) needles.
Beg with a k row, cont in st st and stripes of 8 rows M and
4 rows C until back measures 12(14:16:19:21:23:25)cm/
4 ¾(5 ½:6 ¼:7 ½:8 ¼:9:9 ¾)in from cast on edge, ending with
a p row **.
Shape armholes
Cast off 4 sts at beg of next 2 rows. 58(62:66:70:74:78:82) sts.
Next row K4, skpo, k to last 6 sts, k2 tog, k4.
Next row P to end.
Rep the last 2 rows until 26(28:30:32:34:36:38) sts rem **at the
same time** when the 2nd stripe in C has been completed after
shaping armholes cont in M only.
Cast off.

FRONT

Work as given for back to **.
Shape armholes
Next row Cast off 6 sts, k to end.
Next row Cast off 4 sts, p to end. 56(60:64:68:72:76:80) sts.
Next row K2, skpo, k to last 6 sts, k2 tog, k4.
Next row P to end.
Rep the last 2 rows until 24(26:28:30:32:34:36) sts rem **at the
same time** when the 2nd stripe in C has been completed after
shaping armholes cont in M only.
Rep the last 2 rows until 24(26:28:30:32:34:36) sts rem.
Cast off.

RIGHT SLEEVE

With 3mm (US 2) needles and C cast on 34(34:38:42:46:46:50) sts.
1st rib row K2, [p2, k2] to end.
2nd rib row P2, [k2, p2] to end.
These 2 rows form the rib.
Work a further 10(10:10:12:12:12:14) rows.
Change to 3.25mm (US 3) needles.
Beg with a k row, cont in st st and stripes of 8 rows M and
4 rows C.
Work 2(2:2:2:2:6:6) rows.
Inc row K3, m1, k to last 3 sts, m1, k3.
Work 5(5:5:5:5:3:3) rows.
Rep the last 6(6:6:6:6:4:4) rows 4(6:7:8:9:11:12) times more,
and then the inc row again. 46(50:56:62:68:72:78) sts.
Cont straight until sleeve measures approx
15(17:19:21:23:25:27)cm/6(6 ¾:7 ½:8 ¼:9:9 ¾:10 ½)in from
cast on edge, ending with the same stripe row as on back to
beg of armhole shaping ***.
Shape sleeve top
Cast off 4 sts at beg of next 2 rows. 38(42:48:54:60:64:70) sts.
Cont in stripe patt until the 2nd stripe in C has been
completed on sleeve top then cont in M only **at the same time
work** raglan shaping as follows:
Next row K4, skpo, k to last 6 sts, k2 tog, k4.
Next row P to end.
Next row K to end.
Next row P to end.
Rep the last 4 rows 4(4:3:2:1:1:0) times more.
3rd, 4th 5th, 6th and 7th sizes only
Next row K4, skpo, k to last 6 sts, k2 tog, k4.
Next row P to end.
Rep the last 2 rows -(-:2:4:7:7:11) times more.
All sizes
Rep the last 2 rows until 16(18:20:22:24:26:28) sts rem.
Cast off.

LEFT SLEEVE

Work as given for right sleeve to ***.
Shape sleeve top
Next row Cast off 4 sts, k to end.
Next row Cast off 6 sts, p to end. 36(40:46:52:58:62:68) sts.
Cont in stripe patt until the 2nd stripe in C has been completed on sleeve top then cont in M only **at the same time work** raglan shaping as follows:
Next row K4, skpo, k to last 4 sts, k2 tog, k2.
Next row P to end.
Next row K to end.
Next row P to end.
Rep the last 4 rows 4(4:3:2:1:1:0) times more.
3rd, 4th 5th, 6th and 7th sizes only
Next row K4, skpo, k to last 4 sts, k2 tog, k2.
Next row P to end.
Rep the last 2 rows -(-:2:4:7:7:11) times more.
All sizes
Rep the last 2 rows until 14(16:18:20:22:24:26) sts rem.
Cast off.

NECKBAND

Join both back and right front raglan seams.
With right side facing, using 3mm (US 2) needles and C, pick up and k22(24:24:26:26:28:30) sts from front neck edge, 14(16:19:21:24:26:28) sts from right sleeve, 24(26:28:30:32:34:36) sts from back neck, 12(14:17:19:22:24:26) sts from left sleeve. 72(80:88:96:104:112:120) sts.
1st row P3, [k2, p2] to last 5 sts, k2, p3.
2nd row K3, [p2, k2] to last 5 sts, p2, k3.
Rep the last 2 rows twice more, and then the 1st row again.
Cast off in rib.

BUTTON BAND

With right side facing, using 3mm (US 2) needles and C pick up and k30(30:34:34:38:38: 42) sts evenly down left sleeve edge.
1st row P2, [k2, p2] to end.
2nd row K2, [p2, k2] to end.
Rep the last 2 rows once more, and then the 1st row again.
Cast off in rib.

BUTTONHOLE BAND

With right side facing, using 3mm (US 2) needles and C pick up and k31(31:35:35:39:39:43) sts evenly up front edge.
1st row P2, [k2, p2] to last 5 sts, k2, p3.
2nd row K3, [p2, k2] to end.
Buttonhole row Rib 3, yrn, rib 2 tog, [rib 8(8:10:10:12:12:16], yrn, rib 2 tog] twice, rib 6.
Rib 2 more rows.
Cast off in rib.

TO MAKE UP

Join side and sleeve seams. Join left under arm seam. Lap buttonhole band over buttonband and sew in place. Sew on buttons.

NILS LEGGINGS

SKILL LEVEL **Improving**

SIZES / MEASUREMENTS

To fit age	0-3	3-6	6-12	12-18	18-24	mths

ACTUAL GARMENT MEASUREMENTS

Over	38	43	48	53	58	cm
nappy	15	17	19	21	23	in
Length	31	34	37	41	45	cm
	12 ¼	13 ½	14 ½	16	17 ¾	in

MATERIALS

2(2:2:2:3) 50g/1 ¾oz balls each of MillaMia Naturally Soft Merino in Fawn (160) (M) and Scarlet (140) (C).
Pair each of 3mm (US 2) and 3.25mm (US 3) knitting needles.
Waist length of elastic.
4 buttons (approx 15mm/½in diameter).

TENSION / GAUGE

25 sts and 34 rows to 10cm/4in square over st st using 3.25mm (US 3) needles.

HINTS AND TIPS

Part of the mix and match set these stripey bottoms are fabulous. Team them with the matching Nils Stripey Top or mix it up with the Jonas Comfy Top. Note that the leggings are worked from the waistband down.

ABBREVIATIONS

See page 9.

SUGGESTED ALTERNATIVE COLOURWAYS

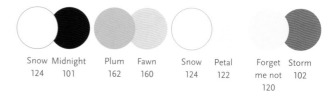

Snow 124 Midnight 101 Plum 162 Fawn 160 Snow 124 Petal 122 Forget me not 120 Storm 102

19 (21 ½ : 24 : 26 ½ : 29) cm
7 ½ (8 ½ : 9 ½ : 10 ½ : 11 ½) in

31 (34 : 37 : 41 : 45) cm
12 ¼ (13 ½ : 14 ½ : 16 : 17 ¾) in

LEFT LEG

With 3mm (US 2) needles and C cast on 50(58:62:70:74) sts.

1st rib row K2, [p2, k2] to end.

2nd rib row P2, [k2, p2] to end.

These 2 rows form the rib.

Work a further 12 rows.

Change to 3.25mm (US 3) needles.

Beg with a k row, cont in st st and stripes of 8 rows M and 4 rows C.

1st row K12(14:16:17:18), turn and work on these sts.

2nd row P to end.

3rd row K to last 2 sts, m1, k2.

4th row P to end.

Rep the last 2 rows 9(10:11:12:13) times more.

22(25:28:30:32) sts.

Break off yarns.

Leave these sts on a holder.

With right side facing rejoin yarn to rem sts.

Cast on 6 sts, k to end, dec 2 sts on 2nd and 4th sizes only.

44(48:52:57:62) sts.

Work 21(23:25:27:29) rows in st st and stripe patt.

Next row K16(17:18:19:20), turn, leave rem 28(31:34:38:42) sts on a holder.

Work 9 rows in st st.

Cast off.

Joining row K22(25:28:30:32) sts on first holder, then k28(31:34:38:42) sts on second holder. 50(56:62:68:74) sts.

✲✲ Cont in st st and stripe patt until work measures 14(15:17:18:20)cm/5 ½(6:6 ¾:7:8)in from cast on edge, ending with a p row.

Shape crotch

Inc row K2, m1, k to last 2 sts, m1, k2.

Next row P to end.

Rep the last 2 rows 4(4:5:5:6) times more. 60(66:74:80:88) sts.

Cast on 3(3:3:4:4) sts at beg of next 2 rows.

66(72:80:88:96) sts.

Shape for legs

Work 2 rows.

Next row K2, skpo, k to last 4 sts, k2 tog, k2.

Next row P to end.

Rep the last 2 rows 4(4:5:6:7) times more. 56(62:68:74:80) sts.

Cont straight until work measures 27(30:33:37:41)cm/10 ¾(11 ¾: 13:14 ½:16)in from cast on edge, ending with a k row.

Cont in C only.

Next row P to end, dec 2(4:2:4:2) sts evenly across row.

54(58:66:70:78) sts.

Change to 3mm (US 2) needles.

1st rib row K2, [p2, k2] to end.

2nd rib row P2, [k2, p2] to end.

These 2 rows form the rib.

Work a further 14 rows.

Cast off in rib.

Pocket edging

With right side facing, using 3mm (US 2) needles and C pick up and k17(17:21:21:25) sts evenly along shaped edge, then cast on 11 sts. 28(28:32:32:36) sts.

1st row K1, [p2, k2] to last 3 sts, p3.

2nd row K3, [p2, k2] to last 5 sts, p2, k3.

These 2 rows form the rib.

Buttonhole row K1, p1, p2 tog, yon, rib 4, yrn, p2 tog, rib to end.

Rib a further 3 rows.

Cast off in rib.

RIGHT LEG

With 3mm (US 2) needles and C cast on 50(58:62:70:74) sts.
1st rib row K2, [p2, k2] to end.
2nd rib row P2, [k2, p2] to end.
These 2 rows form the rib.
Work a further 12 rows.
Change to 3.25mm (US 3) needles.
Beg with a k row, cont in st st and stripes of 8 rows M and 4 rows C.
1st row K across 38(44:46:53:56) sts, dec 2 sts on 2nd and 4th sizes only, turn and cast on 6 sts, p to end. 44(48:52:57:62) sts.
Work 20(22:24:26:28) rows in st st and stripe patt.
Next row K28(31:34:38:42), leave these sts on a holder, k to end. 16(17:18:19:20) sts.
Work 9 rows in st st.
Cast off.
With right side facing rejoin yarn to rem 12(14:16:17:18) sts.
1st row K to end.
2nd row P to end.
3rd row K2, m1, k to end.
4th row P to end.
Rep the last 2 rows 9(10:11:12:13) times more.
22(25:28:30:32) sts.
Next row K to end.
Joining row P22(25:28:30:32), then p28(31:34:38:42) sts from first holder.
Work as given for left leg from ** to end.
Pocket edging
With right side facing, using 3mm (US 2) needles and C cast on 11 sts, pick up and k17(17:21:21:25) sts evenly along shaped edge. 28(28:32:32:36) sts.
1st row P3, [k2, p2] to last st, k1.
2nd row K3, [p2, k2] to last 5 sts, p2, k3.
These 2 rows form the rib.
Buttonhole row Rib to last 10 sts, p2 tog, yon, rib 4, yrn, p2 tog, p1, k1.
Rib a further 3 rows.
Cast off in rib.

MAKE UP

Sew pockets in place. Join inner leg seams. Join centre front and back seam. Sew cast on edge of pocket edgings to waistband. Sew on buttons. Join elastic into a ring. Work a herringbone casing over rib at waist, enclosing elastic.

JONAS COMFY TOP

SKILL LEVEL **Beginner / Improving**

SIZES / MEASUREMENTS

To fit age	0-3	3-6	6-12	12-18	18-24	24-36	mths

ACTUAL GARMENT MEASUREMENTS

Chest	51	54	58	61	64	67	cm
	20	21 ¼	23	24	25	26 ½	in
Length to	25	28	31	35	38	41	cm
shoulder	9 ¾	11	12 ¼	13 ¾	15	16 ¼	in
Sleeve	15	17	19	21	23	25	cm
length	6	6 ¾	7 ½	8 ¼	9	9 ¾	in

MATERIALS

3(4:5:6:6:7) 50g/1 ¾oz balls of MillaMia Naturally Soft Merino in Seaside (161) (M).
One ball of Midnight (101) (C).
Pair each of 3mm (US 2) and 3.25mm (US 3) knitting needles.

TENSION / GAUGE

25 sts and 34 rows to 10cm/4in square over st st using 3.25mm (US 3) needles.

HINTS AND TIPS

Part of our mix and match collection this hooded top looks as good with the Nils Leggings as the Jonas Comfy Bottoms – or for older boys with jeans. Block the pocket and front piece nice and flat before you sew the pocket on and pin it in place first so that it is well positioned before you start sewing.

ABBREVIATIONS

See page 9.

SUGGESTED ALTERNATIVE COLOURWAYS

Fawn 160 Scarlet 140 Plum 162 Fawn 160 Snow 124 Petal 122 Forget me not 120 Storm 102

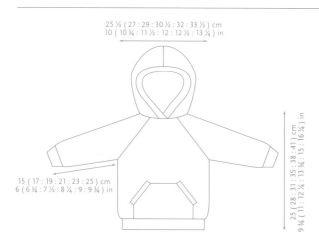

25 ½ (27 : 29 : 30 ½ : 32 : 33 ½) cm
10 (10 ¾ : 11 ½ : 12 : 12 ½ : 13 ¼) in

15 (17 : 19 : 21 : 23 : 25) cm
6 (6 ¾ : 7 ½ : 8 ¼ : 9 : 9 ¾) in

25 (28 : 31 : 35 : 38 : 41) cm
9 ¾ (11 : 12 ¼ : 13 ¾ : 15 : 16 ¼) in

BACK and FRONT (alike)

With 3mm (US 2) needles and C, cast on 68(68:74:80:80:86) sts.
1st rib row K3, [p2, k4] to last 5 sts, p2, k3.
2nd rib row P3, [k2, p4] to last 5 sts, k2, p3.
These 2 rows form the rib.
Work a further 10(10:12:12:14:14) rows, dec(inc:-:dec:inc:-)
2(2:0:2:2:0) sts evenly across last row. 66(70:74:78:82:86) sts.
Cut off C.
Join on M.
Change to 3.25mm (US 3) needles.
Beg with a k row, cont in st st until back measures
12(14:16:19:21:23)cm/4 ¾(5 ½:6 ¼:7 ½:8 ¼:9)in from cast on
edge, ending with a p row.
Shape armholes
Cast off 4 sts at beg of next 2 rows. 58(62:66:70:74:78) sts.
Next row K4, skpo, k to last 6 sts, k2 tog, k4.
Next row P to end.
Rep the last 2 rows until 26(28:30:32:34:36) sts rem.
Cast off.

SLEEVES

With 3mm (US 2) needles and C cast on 34(34:38:42:46:46) sts.
1st rib row K2, [p2, k2] to end.
2nd rib row P2, [k2, p2] to end.
These 2 rows form the rib.
Work a further 10(10:12:12:14:14) rows.
Cut off C.
Join on M.
Change to 3.25mm (US 3) needles.
Beg with a k row, cont in st st.
Work 6 rows.
Inc row K3, m1, k to last 3 sts, m1, k3.
Work 3 rows.
Rep the last 4 rows 4(6:7:8:9:11) times more, and then the inc
row again. 46(50:56:62:68:72) sts.

Cont straight until sleeve measures 15(17:19:21:23:25)cm/
6(6 ¾:7 ½:8 ¼:9:9 ¾)in from cast on edge, ending with a p row.
Shape sleeve top
Cast off 4 sts at beg of next 2 rows. 38(42:48:54:60:64) sts.
Next row K4, skpo, k to last 6 sts, k2 tog, k4.
Next row P to end.
Next row K to end.
Next row P to end.
Rep the last 4 rows 4(4:3:2:1:1) times more.
Next row K4, skpo, k to last 6 sts, k2 tog, k4.
Next row P to end.
Rep the last 2 rows until 16(18:20:22:24:26) sts rem.
Cast off.

POCKET

With 3.25mm (US 3) needles and M, cast on
40(44:48:52:56:60) sts.
Beg with a k row work 18(20:22:24:26:28) rows in st st.
Shape top
Next row K1, skpo, k to last 3 sts, k2 tog, k1.
Next row P to end.
Rep the last 2 rows until 20(22:24:26:28:30) sts rem.
Cast off.
Edgings
With right side facing, using 3mm (US 2) needles and C pick
up and k20(20:24:24:28:28) sts evenly along shaped edge.
1st row P3, [k2, p2] to last 5 sts, k2, p3.
2nd row K3, [p2, k2] to last 5 sts, p2, k3.
Rep the last 2 rows twice more, and then the 1st row again.
Cast off in rib.

HOOD

With 3.25mm (US 3) needles and M, cast on
78(86:94:102:110:118) sts.
Beg with a k row cont in st st until hood measures
16(17:18:19:20:21)cm/6 ¼ (6 ¾:7:7 ½:8:8 ¼)in, ending with a
p row.
Shape top
Next row K36(40:44:48:52:56), k2 tog, k2, skpo, k to end.
Next row P to end.
Next row K35(39:43:47:51:55), k2 tog, k2, skpo, k to end.
Next row P to end.
Next row K34(38:42:46:50:54), k2 tog, k2, skpo, k to end.
Next row P to end.
Next row K33(37:41:45:49:53), k2 tog, k2, skpo, k to end.
Next row P to end.
Next row K32(36:40:44:48:52), k2 tog, k2, skpo, k to end.
Next row P to end.
Next row K31(35:39:43:47:51), k2 tog, k2, skpo, k to end.
Next row P to end.
Next row K33(37:41:45:49:53), turn and work on these sts.
Cast off 6(7:8:9:10:11) sts at beg of next and 3 foll wrong side rows.
Work 1 row.
Cast off rem 9 sts.
With right side facing rejoin yarn to rem sts, cast off
6(7:8:9:10:11) sts, k to end.
Next row P to end.
Cast off 6(7:8:9:10:11) sts at beg of next and 2 foll right side
rows.
Work 1 row.
Cast off rem 9 sts.

EDGING

Join top seam of hood.
With right side facing, using 3mm (US 2) needles and C pick
up and k116(120:128:132:140:148) sts evenly along row ends.
1st row P3, [k2, p2] to last 5 sts, k2, p3.
2nd row K3, [p2, k2] to last 5 sts, p2, k3.
Rep the last 2 rows twice, and then the 1st row again.
Cast off in rib.

TO MAKE UP

Join raglan seams. Lap right side of hood border over left,
place border at centre front, then sew hood in place, easing in
fullness. Join side and sleeve seams. Sew on pocket.

JONAS COMFY BOTTOMS

SKILL LEVEL **Beginner**

SIZES / MEASUREMENTS

To fit age	0-3	3-6	6-12	12-18	18-24	mths

ACTUAL GARMENT MEASUREMENTS

Over nappy	38	43	48	53	58	cm
	15	17	19	21	23	in
Length	30	33	36	40	44	cm
	11 ¾	13	14	15 ¾	17 ½	in

MATERIALS

2(2:2:3:4) 50g/1 ¾oz balls of MillaMia Naturally Soft Merino in Fawn (160) (M).
One ball of Scarlet (140) (C).
Pair each of 3mm (US 2) and 3.25mm (US 3) knitting needles.
Waist length of elastic.

TENSION / GAUGE

25 sts and 34 rows to 10cm/4in square over st st using 3.25mm (US 3) needles.

HINTS AND TIPS

Super comfortable and relaxed these yoga style trousers are perfect for slouching around in. Also part of the mix and match Nils and Jonas sets, these bottoms look great with either or both the Nils and Jonas tops. The elastic incorporated around the waist makes sure the trousers stay put and the bow on the front is a decorative addition.

ABBREVIATIONS

See page 9.

SUGGESTED ALTERNATIVE COLOURWAYS

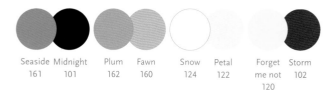

Seaside	Midnight	Plum	Fawn	Snow	Petal	Forget me not	Storm
161	101	162	160	124	122	120	102

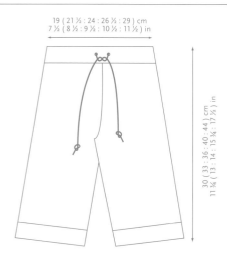

19 (21 ½ : 24 : 26 ½ : 29) cm
7 ½ (8 ½ : 9 ½ : 10 ½ : 11 ½) in

30 (33 : 36 : 40 : 44) cm
11 ¾ (13 : 14 : 15 ¾ : 17 ½) in

LEGS (make 2)

With 3mm (US 2) needles and C cast on 50(56:62:68:74) sts.
1st rib row K3, [p2, k4] to last 5 sts, p2, k3.
2nd rib row P3, [k2, p4] to last 5 sts, k2, p3.
These 2 rows form the rib.
Work a further 10(10:12:12:14) rows.
Cut off C.
Join on M.
Change to 3.25mm (US 3) needles.
Beg with a k row, cont in st st until work measures
14(15:17:18:20)cm/5 ½(6:6 ¾:7:8)in from cast on edge,
ending with a p row.
Shape crotch
Inc row K2, m1, k to last 2 sts, m1, k2.
Next row P to end.
Rep the last 2 rows 4(4:5:5:6) times more. 60(66:74:80:88) sts.
Cast on 3(3:3:4:4) sts at beg of next 2 rows. 66(72:80:88:96) sts.
Shape for legs
Work 2 rows.
Next row K2, skpo, k to last 4 sts, k2 tog, k2.
Next row P to end.
Rep the last 2 rows 4(4:5:6:7) times more. 56(62:68:74:80) sts.
Cont straight until work measures 27(30:33:37:41)cm/10 ¾(11 ¾:
13:14 ½:16)in from cast on edge, ending with a k row.
Cut off M.
Join on C.
Next row P to end.
Change to 3mm (US 2) needles.
1st rib row K3, [p2, k4] to last 5 sts, p2, k3.
2nd rib row P3, [k2, p4] to last 5 sts, k2, p3.
These 2 rows form the rib.
Work a further 8 rows.
Cast off in rib.

MAKE UP

Join inner leg seams on each leg. Sew two legs together by joining centre front and back seam. Join elastic into a ring. Work a herringbone casing over rib at waist, enclosing elastic. Using C make 2 twisted cords and attach to centre front for the decorative tie.

To make twisted cords (make 2)

Start with a piece of yarn at least four times as long as you want the finished length to be. Fold the yarn in half and hold the two loose ends tightly between two fingers of your left (or non-dominant hand). Put the index finger of your other hand in the loop at the other end of the yarn and circle your hand so that the yarn twists. Keep twisting until it is tight against the finger in the loop. Ease your finger out of the loop and carefully, without letting go of the other end, match up the two ends of the twisted piece of yarn and hold it tightly between your fingers. Let go of the doubled end of the yarn – the cord should begin to form on its own. Smooth it out so that the twists are even and tightly knot the loose ends.

KLARA
KIMONO
FILIPPA
DRESS
FILIP
TANK TOP

From left to right: **Filip Tank Top** in Midnight (101), Forget me not (120),
Snow (124), Grass (141), Scarlet (140), Seaside (161), Moss (103), Storm (102),
Claret (104), and Lilac Blossom (123) pattern on page 72,
Klara Kimono and **Filippa Dress** in Storm (102), Snow (124), Claret (104),
Petal (122), Fuchsia (143), Forget me not (120), Midnight (101), Daisy Yellow (142),
Grass (141) and Lilac Blossom (123) patterns on pages 60 and 66 respectively

KLARA KIMONO

SKILL LEVEL **Experienced**

SIZES / MEASUREMENTS

To fit age	6-12	12-18	18-24	24-36	36-48	mths

ACTUAL GARMENT MEASUREMENTS

Chest	50	54	56	60	63	cm
	19 ¾	21 ½	22	23 ½	24 ¾	in
Length to	30 ½	34	37	41	45	cm
shoulder	12	13 ½	14 ½	16	17 ¾	in
Sleeve	17	19	21	24	27	cm
length	6 ¾	7 ½	8 ¼	9 ½	10 ¾	in

MATERIALS

Two 50g/1 ¾oz balls of MillaMia Naturally Soft Merino in Storm (102) (M).
1(1:2:2:2) balls of Snow (124).
One ball in each of Claret (104), Petal (122), Fuchsia (143), Forget me not (120), Midnight (101), Daisy Yellow (142), Grass (141) and Lilac Blossom (123).
Pair each of 3mm (US 2) and 3.25mm (US 3) knitting needles.
Four buttons (approx 15 mm/½in diameter).

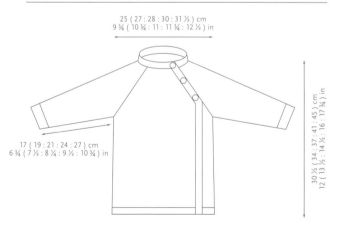

25 (27 : 28 : 30 : 31 ½) cm
9 ¾ (10 ¾ : 11 : 11 ¾ : 12 ½) in

17 (19 : 21 : 24 : 27) cm
6 ¾ (7 ½ : 8 ¼ : 9 ½ : 10 ¾) in

30 ½ (34 : 37 : 41 : 45) cm
12 (13 ½ : 14 ½ : 16 : 17 ¾) in

TENSION / GAUGE

25 sts and 34 rows to 10cm/4in square over st st using 3.25mm (US 3) needles.

HINTS AND TIPS

An interesting and challenging project, this kimono involves a bit of shaping to achieve the asymmetrical front while concurrently working on the Fair Isle pattern. Please note this is more complicated than a traditional Fair Isle in that more than two colours are used at once at some points. Make sure not to strand the yarn you are carrying behind the work too tightly or the pattern will pucker and the garment may end up too narrow. A thin button band sits behind the right front to help secure the left front in place but is not visible once the kimono is on. You may want to colour photocopy and enlarge the chart so that you can annotate your progress.

ABBREVIATIONS

See page 9.

SUGGESTED ALTERNATIVE COLOURWAY

| Midnight 101 | Snow 124 | Moss 103 | Seaside 161 | Scarlet 140 | Forget me not 120 | Storm 102 | Claret 104 | Grass 141 | Lilac Blossom 123 |

NOTE

Back and sleeves When working from Chart read rows from right to left, after working the centre st (last st on left hand side – marked C) read the chart from left to right, omitting the centre st.
Fronts When working from Chart, start where indicated for right side rows to centre st reading from right to left, then after working centre st, read the chart from left to right, omitting the centre st and make a note of where you finish. Start wrong side rows here working from left to right.

BACK

With 3mm (US 2) needles and M cast on 65(69:73:77:81) sts.
1st rib row P1, [k1, p1] to end.
2nd rib row K1, [p1, k1] to end.
Rep the last 2 rows twice more.
Change to 3.25mm (US 3) needles.
Beg with a k row, work in st st and patt from Chart until back measures 17(19:21:24:27)cm/6 ¾(7 ½:8 ¼:9 ½:10 ¾)in from cast on edge, ending with a p row.
Shape raglan armholes
Cast off 4 sts at beg of next 2 rows. 57(61:65:69:73) sts.
Next row Skpo, patt to last 2 sts, k2 tog.
Next row Patt to end.
Next row Patt to end.
Next row Patt to end.
Rep the last 4 rows once more. 53(57:61:65:69) sts.
Next row Skpo, patt to last 2 sts, k2 tog.
Next row Patt to end.
Rep the last 2 rows 13(14:15:16:17) times more. 25(27:29:31:33) sts.
Leave these sts on a holder.

LEFT FRONT

With 3mm (US 2) needles and M cast on 29(29:31:31:33) sts.
1st rib row K1, [p1, k1] to end.
2nd rib row K2, p1, [k1, p1] to end.
Rep the last 2 rows once more, and then the 1st row again.
Next row Rib 8, leave these sts on a holder, inc 0(1:0:1:0) sts, rib to end. 21(22:23:24:25) sts.
Change to 3.25mm (US 3) needles.
Beg with a k row, work in st st and patt from Chart until front measures 17(19:21:24:27)cm/6 ¾(7 ½:8 ¼:9 ½:10 ¾)in from cast on edge, ending with a p row.
Shape raglan armhole
Next row Cast off 4 sts, patt to end. 17(18:19:20:21) sts.
Next row Patt to end.

Next row Skpo, patt to end.
Next row Patt to end.
Next row Patt to end.
Next row Patt to end.
Rep the last 4 rows once more. 15(16:17:18:19) sts.
Next row Skpo, patt to end.
Next row Patt to end.
Rep the last 2 rows 13(14:15:16:17) times more. 1 st.
Fasten off.

RIGHT FRONT

With 3mm (US 2) needles and M cast on 57(59:63:65:69) sts.
1st rib row K1, [p1, k1] to end.
2nd rib row P1, [k1, p1] to last 2 sts, k2.
Rep the last 2 rows once more, and then the 1st row again.
Next row Inc 0(1:0:1:0) sts at centre of row, rib to last 8 sts, place these 8 sts on a holder. 49(52:55:58:61) sts.
Change to 3.25mm (US 3) needles.
Beg with a k row, work in st st and patt from Chart until front measures 17(19:21:24:27)cm/6 ¾(7 ½:8 ¼:9 ½:10 ¾)in from cast on edge, ending with a k row.
Shape raglan armhole
Next row Cast off 4 sts, patt to end. 45(48:51:54:57) sts.
Next row Patt to last 2 sts, k2 tog.
Next row Patt to end.
Next row Patt to end.
Next row Patt to end.
Rep the last 4 rows once more. 43(46:49:52:55) sts.
Next row Patt to last 2 sts, k2 tog.
Next row Patt to end.
Rep the last 2 rows 3(4:5:6:7) times more. 39(41:43:45:47) sts.
Next row Skpo, patt to last 2 sts, k2 tog.
Next row Patt to end.
Rep the last 2 rows 9 times more. 19(21:23:25:27) sts.
Leave these sts on a holder.

CHART

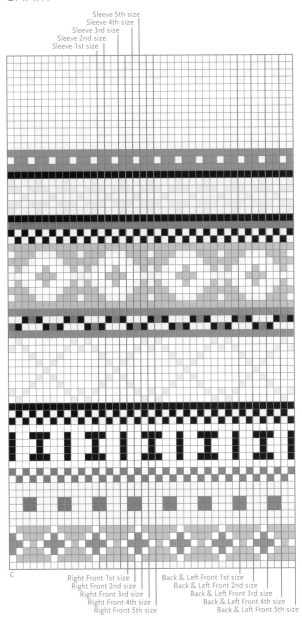

Sleeve 5th size
Sleeve 4th size
Sleeve 3rd size
Sleeve 2nd size
Sleeve 1st size

Key

Lilac Blossom (123)
Daisy Yellow (142)
Midnight (101)
Claret (104)
Petal (122)
Fuchsia (143)
Grass (141)
Storm (102)
Forget me not (120)
Snow (124)
C Centre st

C

Right Front 1st size
Right Front 2nd size
Right Front 3rd size
Right Front 4th size
Right Front 5th size

Back & Left Front 1st size
Back & Left Front 2nd size
Back & Left Front 3rd size
Back & Left Front 4th size
Back & Left Front 5th size

SLEEVES

With 3mm (US 2) needles and M cast on 25(27:31:35:37) sts.
1st rib row K1, [p1, k1] to end.
2nd rib row P1, [k1, p1] to end.
Rep the last 2 rows twice more.
Change to 3.25mm (US 3) needles.
Beg with a k row, cont in st st and patt from Chart.
Work 2 rows.
Inc and work into patt one st at each end of the next and every foll 4th row until there are 49(55:61:69:75) sts.
Cont straight until sleeve measures 17(19:21:24:27)cm/6 ¾(7 ½: 8 ¼:9 ½:10 ¾)in from cast on edge, ending with a p row.
Shape raglan armholes
Cast off 4 sts at beg of next 2 rows. 41(47:53:61:67) sts.
1st, 2nd, 3rd and 4th sizes only
Next row Skpo, patt to last 2 sts, k2 tog.
Next row Patt to end.
Next row Patt to end.
Next row Patt to end.
Rep the last 4 rows 3(2:1:0:-) times more. 33(41:49:59:67) sts.
All sizes
Next row Skpo, patt to last 2 sts, k2 tog.
Next row Patt to end.
Rep the last 2 rows 9(12:15:18:21) times more.
13(15:17:21:23) sts.
Leave these sts on a holder.

LEFT FRONT BAND

With right side facing, using 3mm (US 2) needles, rejoin M to sts on holder, cast on one st, rib to end. 9 sts.
Cont in rib, as set, until band fits along straight edge of front, ending with a wrong side row.
Leave these sts on a holder.

RIGHT FRONT BAND

With wrong side facing, using 3mm (US 2) needles, rejoin M to sts on holder, cast on one st, rib to end. 9sts.
Cont in rib, as set, until band fits along straight edge of front, ending with a wrong side row.
Buttonhole row Rib 4, yrn, work 2 tog, rib 3.
Work a further 11 rows.
Rep the last 12 rows once more. Do not cut yarn.

NECKBAND

With right side facing using 3mm (US 2) needles, holding right front band and M, work rib 4, yrn, work 2 tog, rib 2, k across right front band, k last st tog with first st of right front, k17(19:21:23:25), k last st tog with first st of right sleeve, k11(13:15:19:21), k last st tog with first st of back, k23(25:27:29:31), k last st tog with first st of left sleeve, k11(13:15:19:21), k last st tog with first st of left front band, rib 8. 83(91:99:111:119) sts.
Work 5 rows in rib as set.
Cast off in rib.

BUTTONBAND

Using 3mm (US 2) needles and M cast on 36(38:40:42:44) sts.
K 1 row,
Buttonhole row K1, k2 tog, yf, k to end.
K 1 row.
Cast off.

MAKE UP

Sew on front bands. Join raglan seams. Join side and sleeve seams. Sew end of buttonband to front edge of left front 3cm/1 ¼in below armhole shaping. Sew 3 buttons on left front to match buttonholes. Sew remaining button to right side seam 3cm/1 ¼in below armhole shaping.

FILIPPA DRESS

SKILL LEVEL **Improving**

SIZES / MEASUREMENTS

To fit age	2-3	3-4	4-5	5-6	6-7	years

ACTUAL GARMENT MEASUREMENTS

Chest	60	65	69	74	79	cm
	24	25½	27	29	31	in
Length to	50	57	62	68	74	cm
shoulder	19 ¾	22 ½	24 ½	26 ¾	29	in

MATERIALS

2(2:3:3:3) 50g/1 ¾oz balls of MillaMia Naturally Soft Merino in Storm (102) (M).
One ball in each of Snow (124), Claret (104), Petal (122), Fuchsia (143), Forget me not (120), Midnight (101), Daisy Yellow (142), Grass (141) and Lilac Blossom (123).
Pair each of 3mm (US 2) and 3.25mm (US 3) knitting needles.

TENSION / GAUGE

25 sts and 34 rows to 10cm/4in square over st st using 3.25mm (US 3) needles.

30 (32 ½ : 34 ½ : 37 : 39 ½) cm
12 (12 ¾ : 13 ½ : 14 ½ : 15 ½) in

50 (57 : 62 : 68 : 74) cm
19 ¾ (22 ½ : 24 ½ : 26 ¾ : 29) in

HINTS AND TIPS

A beautiful, slim fitting Fair Isle dress. Make sure that you do not strand the thread you are carrying too tight when knitting this item as this is a common risk with Fair Isle work. This may result in too tight a dress. Please note this is more complicated than a traditional Fair Isle in that more than two colours are used at once at some points. The stranding also creates a slightly thicker fabric making this warm and snug. Team it with a simple t-shirt – either long or short sleeved. You may want to colour photocopy and enlarge the chart so that you can annotate your progress.

ABBREVIATIONS

S2kpo – slip next 2 sts as if to k2 tog, k1, then pass 2 slipped sts over.
See also page 9.

SUGGESTED ALTERNATIVE COLOURWAY

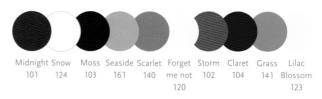

Midnight	Snow	Moss	Seaside	Scarlet	Forget me not	Storm	Claret	Grass	Lilac Blossom
101	124	103	161	140	120	102	104	141	123

NOTE

When working from Chart all rows are read from right to left, after working the centre st (last st on left hand side – marked C) read the chart from left to right, omitting the centre st.

BACK

With 3.25mm (US 3) needles and M cast on 74(80:86:92:98) sts.
1st row P2, [k4, p2] to end.
2nd row K2, [p4, k2] to end.
Rep the last 2 rows 3(3:4:4:5:5) times more, inc 3 sts evenly across last row. 77(83:89:95:101) sts.
Beg with a k row cont in st st.
Work 6(8:10:12:14) rows.
Now work patt from Chart.
Work straight until back measures 40(45:50:55:60)cm/15 ¾(17 ¾: 19 ¾:21 ¾:23 ¾)in from cast on edge, ending with a wrong side row.
Mark each end of last row with a coloured thread.
Shape cap sleeves
Next row K1, m1, patt to last st, m1, k1.
Work 3 rows.
Rep the last 4 rows 6(7:7:8:9) times. 91(99:105:113:121) sts.
Shape upper sleeves
Cast off 5(5:5:6:6) sts at beg of next 6 rows and 5(7:8:7:9) sts at beg of foll 2 rows.
Shape shoulders
Cast off 10(11:12:13:14) sts at beg of foll 2 rows.
Cast off rem 31(33:35:37:39) sts.

FRONT

Work as given for back until 12 rows less have been worked to cap sleeve shaping.
Shape front neck
Next row Patt 36(39:42:45:48), work 2 tog, turn and work on these sts for first side of neck.
Next row Patt to end.
Next row Patt to last 2 sts, work 2 tog.
Rep the last 2 rows 4 times more, and then the 1st row again.
Mark side edge of last row with a coloured thread.

Next row K1, m1, patt to last 2 sts, work 2 tog.
Inc at side edge on next 6(7:7:8:9) foll 4th rows **at the same time** dec one st at neck edge on 8(9:10:11:12) foll alt rows then keep neck edge straight.
Work 3 rows after last inc at side edge, ending at side edge.
Shape upper sleeve
Cast off 5(5:5:6:6) sts at beg of next and 2 foll right side rows.
Work 1 row.
Cast off 5(7:8:7:9) sts at beg of next row.
Work 1 row.
Shape shoulder
Cast off rem 10(11:12:13:14) sts.
With right side facing place centre st on a safety pin, rejoin yarn to rem sts, work 2 tog, patt to end.
Next row Patt to end.
Next row Work 2 tog, patt to end.
Rep the last 2 rows 4 times more, and then the 1st row again.
Mark side edge of last row with a coloured thread.
Next row Work 2 tog, patt to last st, m1, k1.
Inc at side edge on next 6(7:7:8:9) foll 4th rows **at the same time** dec one st at neck edge on 8(9:10:11:12) foll alt rows then keep neck edge straight.
Work 4 rows after last inc at side edge, ending at side edge.
Shape upper sleeve
Cast off 5(5:5:6:6) sts at beg of next and 2 foll wrong side rows.
Work 1 row.
Cast off 5(7:8:7:9) sts at beg of next row.
Work 1 row.
Shape shoulder
Cast off rem 10(11:12:13:14) sts.

CHART

Key

- Lilac Blossom (123)
- Daisy Yellow (142)
- Midnight (101)
- Claret (104)
- Petal (122)
- Fuchsia (143)
- Grass (141)
- Storm (102)
- Forget me not (120)
- Snow (124)
- C Centre st

1st size
2nd size
3rd size
4th size
5th size

C

NECKBAND

Join right shoulder seam.

With right side facing, using 3mm (US 2) needles and M, pick up and k44(48:50:54:56) sts evenly down left side of front neck, k1 from safety pin, pick up and k44(46:50:52:56) sts evenly up right side of front neck, then 28(30:32:34:36) sts from back neck. 117(125:133:141:149) sts.

1st, 2nd and 5th sizes only

1st row [P2, k2] 18(19:-:-:23) times, p1, [k2, p2] to end.

3rd and 4th sizes only

1st row [K2, p2] –(-:20:21:-) times, k2, p1, [p2, k2] to end.

All sizes

This row sets the rib.

2nd row Rib 43(47:49:53:55), s2kpo, rib to end.

3rd row Rib to end.

4th row Rib 42(46:48:52:54), s2kpo, rib to end.

5th row Rib to end.

6th row Rib 41(45:47:51:53), s2kpo, rib to end.

7th row Rib to end.

Cast off in rib, dec on this row as before.

SLEEVE EDGINGS

Join left shoulder seam and neckband.

With 3mm (US 2) needles and M, pick up and k54(58:66:70:78) sts evenly between coloured threads.

1st row P2, [k2, p2] to end.

2nd row K2, [p2, k2] to end.

Rep the last 2 rows once more.

Cast off in rib.

TO MAKE UP

Join side and sleeve edging seams.

FILIP TANK TOP

SKILL LEVEL **Improving**

SIZES / MEASUREMENTS

To fit age	3-6	6-12	12-24	24-36	36-48	48-60	mths

ACTUAL GARMENT MEASUREMENTS

Chest	42	47	52	56	61	66	cm
	16 ½	18 ½	20 ½	22	24	26	in
Length to	25	27	30	33	37	41	cm
shoulder	10	10 ½	11 ¾	13	14 ½	16	in

MATERIALS

1(1:1:2:2:2) 50g balls of MillaMia Naturally Soft Merino in Midnight 101 (M).
One ball in each of Forget me not (120), Snow (124), Grass (141), Scarlet (140), Seaside (161), Moss (103), Storm (102), Claret (104) and Lilac Blossom (123).
Pair each of 3mm (US 2) and 3.25mm (US 3) knitting needles.

TENSION / GAUGE

25 sts and 34 rows to 10cm/4in square over st st using 3.25mm (US 3) needles.

HINTS AND TIPS

A great project to progress your colourwork skills with but please note this is more complicated than a traditional Fair Isle in that more than two colours are used at once at some points. No sleeves and manageable row lengths mean you will quicker master this art though. As with all Fair Isle projects – make sure you do not pull the yarn you are stranding behind the work too tightly. This will result in the pattern puckering and the item coming up smaller than it should be.

ABBREVIATIONS

S2kpo - slip next 2 sts as if to k2 tog, k1, then pass 2 slipped sts over.
See also page 9.

SUGGESTED ALTERNATIVE COLOURWAY

Storm 102	Forget me not 120	Snow 124	Grass 141	Fuchsia 143	Petal 122	Claret 104	Midnight 101	Daisy Yellow 142	Lilac BLossom 123

NOTE

When working from Chart all rows are read from right to left, after working the centre st (last st on left hand side – marked C) read the chart from left to right, omitting the centre st.

21 (23 ½ : 26 : 28 : 30 ½ : 33) cm
8 ¼ (9 ¼ : 10 ¼ : 11 : 12 : 13) in

25 (27 : 30 : 33 : 37 : 41) cm
10 (10 ½ : 11 ¾ : 13 : 14 ½ : 16) in

BACK

With 3mm (US 2) needles and M, cast on 54(58:66:70:78:82) sts.
1st rib row K2, [p2, k2] to end.
2nd rib row P2, [k2, p2] to end.
Rep the last 2 rows 3(3:4:4:5:5) times more, inc 1(3:1:3:1:3) sts evenly across last row. 55(61:67:73:79:85) sts.
Change to 3.25mm (US 3) needles.
Work in patt from Chart until back measures 15(16:18:20:23:26)cm/6(6 ¼:7:8:9:10 ¼)in from cast on edge, ending with a p row.
Shape armholes
Cast off 5 sts at beg of next 2 rows. 45(51:57:63:69:75) sts **.
Next row Skpo, patt to last 2 sts, k2 tog.
Next row Patt to end.
Rep the last 2 rows 2(3:4:5:6:7) times. 39(43:47:51:55:59) sts.
Cont in st st until back measures 25(27:30:33:37:41)cm/10(10 ½: 11 ¾:13:14 ½:16)in from cast on edge, ending with a p row.
Shape shoulders
Cast off 7(8:9:10:11:12) sts at beg of next 2 rows.
25(27:29:31:33:35) sts.
Cast off.

FRONT

Work as given for back to **.
Shape front neck
Next row Skpo, patt 18(21:24:27:30:33), k2 tog, turn and work on these sts for first side of front neck.
Next row Patt to end.
Next row Skpo, patt to last 2 sts, k2 tog.
Rep the last 2 rows 1(2:3:4:5:6) times. 16(17:18:19:20:21) sts.
Keeping armhole edge straight cont to dec at neck edge on 6(6:4:4:4:4) foll alt rows then every foll 4th row until 7(8:9:10:11:12) sts rem.
Cont straight until front measures same as back to shoulder, ending at armhole edge.
Shape shoulder
Cast off.
With right side facing, slip centre st onto a safety pin, join on yarn to rem sts.
Next row Skpo patt to last 2 sts, k2 tog.
Next row Patt to end.
Next row Skpo patt to last 2 sts, k2 tog.
Rep the last 2 rows 1(2:3:4:5:6) times. 16(17:18:19:20:21) sts.
Keeping armhole edge straight cont to dec at neck edge on 6(6:4:4:4:4) foll alt rows then every foll 4th row until 7(8:9:10:11:12) sts rem.
Cont straight until front measures same as back to shoulder, ending at armhole edge.
Shape shoulder
Cast off.

CHART

Lilac Blossom (123)
Claret (104)
Storm (102)
Moss (103)
Seaside (161)
Scarlet (140)
Grass (141)
Midnight (101)
Forget me not (120)
Snow (124)
C Centre st

1st size 2nd size 3rd size 4th size 5th size 6th size

C

NECKBAND

Join right shoulder seam.

With right side facing, using 3mm (US 2) needles and M, pick up and k32(36:38:42:44:48) sts evenly down left side of front neck, k1 from safety pin, pick up and k32(34:38:40:44:46) sts evenly up right side of front neck, then 28(30:32:34:36:38) sts from back. 93(101:109:117:125:133) sts.

1st, 2nd, 5th and 6th sizes only

1st row [P2, k2] 15(16:-:-:20:21) times, p1, [k2, p2] to end.

3rd and 4th sizes only

1st row [K2, p2] -(-:17:18:-:-) times, k2, p1, k2, [p2, k2] to end.

All sizes

This row sets the rib.

2nd row Rib 31(35:37:41:43:47), s2kpo, rib to end.

3rd row Rib to end.

4th row Rib 30(34:36:40:42:46), s2kpo, rib to end.

5th row Rib to end.

4th, 5th and 6th sizes only

6th row Rib -(-:-:39:41:45), s2kpo, rib to end.

7th row Rib to end.

8th row Rib -(-:-:38:40:44), s2kpo, rib to end.

9th row Rib to end.

All sizes

Cast off in rib, dec on this row as before.

ARMBANDS

Join left shoulder seam and neckband.

With right side facing, using 3mm (US 2) needles and M, pick up and k78(82:86:94:98:102) sts evenly around armhole edge.

1st row P2, [k2, p2] to end.

2nd row K2, [p2, k2] to end.

These 2 rows set the rib patt.

Work a further 3(3:5:5:7:7) rows.

Cast off in rib.

TO MAKE UP

Join side and armband seams.

FIA HAT & SCARF

SKILL LEVEL **Scarf – Beginner / Hat – Improving**

ACTUAL MEASUREMENTS

Scarf   13cm/5in wide by 110cm/43 ¼in long

Hat   First size to fit Baby (0-1 years)
Second size to fit Toddler (1-3 years)

MATERIALS

Scarf Three 50g/1 ¾oz balls of MillaMia Naturally Soft Merino in Lilac Blossom (123) (M).
One ball in each of Snow (124), Petal (122), Fuchsia (143), Forget me not (120), Midnight (101), Daisy Yellow (142) and Storm (102).
Pair of 3.25mm (US 3) needles.

Hat 1(2) balls Lilac Blossom (123) (M).
One ball in each of Snow (124), Petal (122), Fuchsia (143), Forget me not (120), Midnight (101), Daisy Yellow (142) and Storm (102).
Pair of 3.25mm (US 3) needles, plus a spare 3.25mm (US 3) needle.
Circular 3.25mm (US 3) needle.

TENSION / GAUGE

25 sts and 34 rows to 10cm/4in over st st using 3.25mm (US 3) needles.

HINTS AND TIPS

So practical with the little ear flaps this is a beautiful set for any child and would make a fabulous gift. And a great way to get into colourwork as the patterns are quite small and achievable. Note that the scarf is knitted flat and then sewn together and pressed flat.

ABBREVIATIONS

m1pw – make 1 purlwise
See also page 9.

SUGGESTED ALTERNATIVE COLOURWAY

| Forget me not 120 | Snow 124 | Seaside 161 | Scarlet 140 | Fawn 160 | Midnight 101 | Grass 141 | Claret 104 |

NOTE

When working from Chart all rows are read from right to left, after working the centre st (last st on left hand side – marked with a C) read the chart from left to right, omitting the centre st.

110 cm / 43 ¼ in

13 cm / 5 in

SCARF

With 3.25mm (US 3) needles and M cast on 65 sts.
Beg with a k row work in st st.
Work 6 rows.
Now work 45 rows from Chart.
Cont in M only until scarf measures 92cm/36 ¼in long, ending with a k row.
Now work 45 rows from Chart.
Cont in M only.
Work 6 rows.
Cast off.

MAKE UP

Join row ends together.
With seam running down centre of back, using 3.25mm (US 3) needles and Storm (102), working through both thicknesses pick up and k34 sts along one short end.
1st row P2, [k2, p2] to end.
2nd row K2, [p2, k2] to end.
Rep the last 2 rows once more, and then the 1st row again.
Cast off in rib.
Work other end to match.

HAT

EAR FLAPS (make 2)

With 3.25mm (US 3) needles and M cast on 6 sts.
Next row P to end.
Next row K1, m1, k to last st, m1, k1.
Next row P1, m1pw, p to last st, m1pw, p1.
Rep the last 2 rows once more. 14 sts.
Next row K2, m1, k to last 2 sts, m1, k2.
Next row P to end.
Rep the last 2 rows 4(5) times more. 24(26) sts.
Next row K to end.
Next row P to end.
Rep the last 2 rows 6(7) times more.
Leave these sts on a holder.

MAIN PART

With a spare 3.25mm (US 3) needle and M, cast on 13(15) sts, break off yarn then onto same needle cast on another 31(35) sts, break off yarn.
With 3.25mm (US 3) needles and M, cast on 13(15) sts, k these 13(15) sts, then k across 24(26) sts of first ear flap, k31(35) sts from spare needle, then k across 24(26) sts of second ear flap, then k13(15) sts from spare needle. 105(117) sts.
Beg with a p row work in st st.
Work 1(5) rows.
Now work 45 rows from Chart.
Cont in M only.
Next row P to end, inc one st at centre on second size only. 105(118) sts.
Shape top
Dec row K1, [skpo, k6(7)] to end. 92(105) sts.
P 1 row.
Dec row K1, [skpo, k5(6)] to end. 79(92) sts.
P 1 row.

CHART

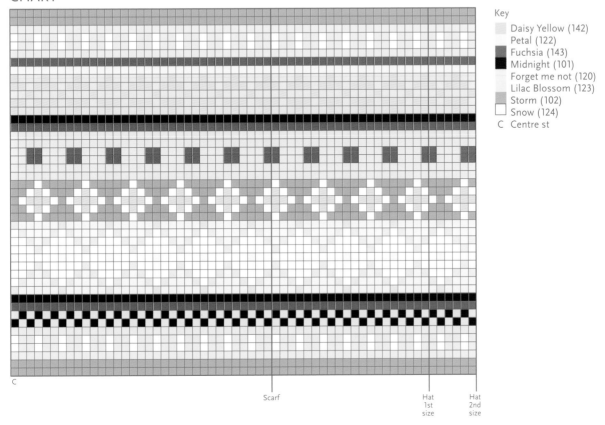

Key

Daisy Yellow (142)
Petal (122)
Fuchsia (143)
Midnight (101)
Forget me not (120)
Lilac Blossom (123)
Storm (102)
Snow (124)
C Centre st

C

Scarf

Hat
1st
size

Hat
2nd
size

Dec row K1, [skpo, k4(5)] to end. 66(79) sts.
P 1 row.
Dec row K1, [skpo, k3(4)] to end. 53(66) sts.
P 1 row.
Dec row K1, [skpo, k2(3)] to end. 40(53) sts.
P 1 row.
Dec row K1, [skpo, k1(2)] to end. 27(40) sts.
P 1 row.
Dec row K1(0), [skpo] to end. 14(20) sts.
P 1 row.
Dec row [Skpo] to end. 7(10) sts.
P 1 row.
Cut off yarn, thread through rem sts, pull up and secure.

EDGING

With right side facing using 3.25mm (US 3) circular needle
and Storm (102) pick up and k13(15) sts along cast on edge
of back, * 13(14) sts along straight edge of earflap, 29(31) sts
around shaped edge of earflap, 13(14) sts along straight edge
of earflap *, 30(34) sts along cast on edge; rep from * to *
once more, 13(15) sts along cast on edge. 166(182) sts.
Work backwards and forwards in rows.
1st row P2, [k2, p2] to end.
2nd row K2, [p2, k2] to end.
Rep the last 2 rows once more, and then the 1st row again.
Cast off in rib.

TIES (make 2)

With 3.25mm (US 3) needles and Storm (102), cast on 7 sts.
1st row K2, p1, k1, p1, k2.
2nd row K1, [p1, k1] 3 times.
Rep the last 2 rows until tie measures 33cm/13in from cast on
edge.
Cast off in rib.

MAKE UP

Join back and edging seam. Sew one tie to each earflap.

LOVISA
CARDIGAN

From left to right: **Lovisa Cardigan**
in Storm (102), Putty Grey (121) and
Fuchsia (143) pattern on page 92
and **Cissi Swing Coat** in Storm (102)
pattern on page 86

CISSI
COAT

CISSI SWING COAT

SKILL LEVEL Beginner / Improving

SIZES / MEASUREMENTS

To fit age	1-2	2-3	4-5	6-7	years

ACTUAL GARMENT MEASUREMENTS

Chest	69	74	78	82	cm
	27	29	30 ¾	32	in
Length to	39	42	45	48	cm
shoulder	15 ¼	16 ½	17 ¾	18 ¾	in
Sleeve length	22	24	27	30	cm
with cuff folded back	8 ¾	9 ½	10 ½	11 ¾	in

MATERIALS

12(13:14:15) 50g/1 ¾oz balls of MillaMia Naturally Soft Merino in Storm (102).
Pair each of 4.50mm (US 7) and 5mm (US 8) knitting needles.
8 buttons (approx 23mm/⅞in diameter).

TENSION / GAUGE

18 sts and 24 rows to 10cm/4in square over st st using 5mm (US 8) needles and yarn double.

HINTS AND TIPS

A 60s inspired swing coat, knitted using the yarn double to produce a warm, thick fabric (with the added benefit of being quick to knit!). The built in scarf is a fun twist on normal designs and has the added benefit that children won't lose it. Dare to try this in bright colours also for a real 60s look. Remember to measure the child before you choose the best size to knit.

ABBREVIATIONS

See page 9.

SUGGESTED ALTERNATIVE COLOURWAYS

Putty Grey	Plum	Fawn	Grass	Midnight	Claret
121	162	160	141	101	104

NOTE

Use yarn double **throughout**.

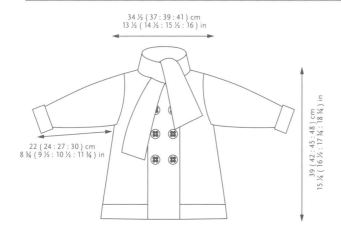

34 ½ (37 : 39 : 41) cm
13 ½ (14 ½ : 15 ½ : 16) in

22 (24 : 27 : 30) cm
8 ¾ (9 ½ : 10 ½ : 11 ¾) in

39 (42 : 45 : 48) cm
15 ¼ (16 ½ : 17 ¾ : 18 ¾) in

BACK

With 4.50mm (US 7) needles and yarn used double cast on 78(82:86:90) sts.
1st and 3rd sizes only
1st row P2, [k2, p2] to end.
2nd row P to end.
2nd and 4th sizes only
1st row K2, [p2, k2] to end.
2nd row P to end.
All sizes
Rep the last 2 rows 6(7:8:9) times more.
Change to 5mm (US 8) needles.
Beg with a k row cont in st st.
Work 2(6:10:12) rows.
Dec row K5, skpo, k to last 7 sts, k2 tog, k5.
Work 5 rows.
Rep the last 6 rows 7 times more. 62(66:70:74) sts.
Shape armholes
Cast off 4 sts at beg of next 2 rows. 54(58:62:66) sts.
Next row K2, skpo, k to last 4 sts, k2 tog, k2.
Next row P to end.
Rep the last 2 rows 2(3:3:4) times more. 48(50:54:56) sts.
Work straight until armhole measures 14(15:16:17)cm/5 ½(6:6 ¼: 6 ¾)in, ending with a wrong side row.
Shape shoulders
Cast off 6(6:7:7) sts at beg of next 2 rows and 7(7:8:8) sts at beg of foll 2 rows.
Cast off rem 22(24:24:26) sts.

LEFT FRONT

With 4.50mm (US 7) needles and yarn used double cast on 33(35:37:39) sts.
1st and 3rd sizes only
1st row P2, [k2, p2] to last 3 sts, k3.
2nd row P to end.
2nd and 4th sizes only
1st row [K2, p2] to last 3 sts, k3.
2nd row P to end.
All sizes
Rep the last 2 rows 6(7:8:9) times more.
Change to 5mm (US 8) needles.
Beg with a k row cont in st st.
Work 2(6:10:12) rows.
Dec row K5, skpo, k to end.
Work 5 rows.
Rep the last 6 rows 7 times more. 25(27:29:31) sts.
Shape armhole
Next row Cast off 4 sts, k to end. 21(23:25:27) sts.
Next row P to end.
Next row K2, skpo, k to end.
Next row P to end.
Rep the last 2 rows 2(3:3:4) times more. 18(19:21:22) sts.
Work straight until 12(14:14:16) rows less have been worked than on back to shoulder shaping, ending with a wrong side row.
Shape neck
Next row K to last 4 sts, k2 tog, k2.
Next row P to end.
Rep the last 2 rows 4(5:5:6) times more. 13(13:15:15) sts.
Work 2 rows.
Shape shoulder
Cast off 6(6:7:7) sts at beg of next row.
Work 1 row.
Cast off rem 7(7:8:8) sts.

RIGHT FRONT

With 4.50mm (US 7) needles and yarn used double cast on 33(35:37:39) sts.

1st and 3rd sizes only
1st row K3, p2, [k2, p2] to end.
2nd row P to end.

2nd and 4th sizes only
1st row K3, [p2, k2] to end.
2nd row P to end.

All sizes
Rep the last 2 rows 6(7:8:9) times more.
Change to 5mm (US 8) needles.
Beg with a k row cont in st st.
Work 2(6:10:12) rows.
Dec row K to last 7 sts, k2 tog, k5.
Work 5 rows.
Rep the last 6 rows 7 times more. 25(27:29:31) sts.
K 1 row.

Shape armhole
Next row Cast off 4 sts, p to end. 21(23:25:27) sts.
Next row K to last 4 sts, k2 tog, k2.
Next row P to end.
Rep the last 2 rows 2(3:3:4) times more. 18(19:21:22) sts.
Work straight until 12(14:14:16) rows less have been worked than on back to shoulder shaping, ending with a wrong side row.

Shape neck
Next row K2, skpo, k to end.
Next row P to end.
Rep the last 2 rows 4(5:5:6) times more. 13(13:15:15) sts.
Work 3 rows.

Shape shoulder
Cast off 6(6:7:7) sts at beg of next row.
Work 1 row.
Cast off rem 7(7:8:8) sts.

SLEEVES

With 5mm (US 8) needles and yarn used double cast on 30(34:38:42) sts.
1st rib row K2, [p2, k2] to end.
2nd rib row P to end.
These 2 rows form the rib.
Work a further 11(11:13:13) rows, ending with a 1st rib row.
Mark each end of last row with a coloured thread.
Change to 4.50mm (US 7) needles.
Beg with a 1st rib row, work a further 12(12:14:14) rows.
Change to 5mm (US 8) needles.
Beg with a k row cont in st st.
Work 2(4:4:6) rows.
Inc row K3, m1, k to last 3 sts, m1, k3.
Work 3 rows.
Rep the last 4 rows 8(8:9:9) times more, and then the inc row again. 50(54:60:64) sts.
Cont straight until sleeve measures 22(24:27:30)cm/8 ¾(9 ½: 10 ½:11 ¾)in from coloured threads, ending with a p row.

Shape armholes
Cast off 4 sts at beg of next 2 rows. 42(46:52:56) sts.
Next row K2, skpo, k to last 4 sts, k2 tog, k2.
Next row P to end.
Rep the last 2 rows 4(5:5:6) times more. 32(34:40:42) sts.
Cast off 3 sts at beg of next 6(6:8:8) rows. 14(16:16:18) sts.
Cast off.

BUTTON BAND

With right side facing, starting at beg of neck shaping,
using 4.50mm (US 7) needles and yarn double, pick up and
k66(70:78:82) sts evenly down left front edge.
1st rib row P to end.
2nd rib row K2, [p2, k2] to end.
Rep the last 2 rows 11 times more, and then the
1st row again.
Cast off in rib.

BUTTONHOLE BAND

With right side facing, ending at beg of neck shaping, using
4.50mm (US 7) needles and yarn double, pick up and
k66(70:78:82) sts evenly up right front edge.
1st rib row P to end.
2nd rib row K2, [p2, k2] to end.
3rd row As 1st row.
Buttonhole row Rib 24(28:36:40), [k2 tog, yrn, rib 10] 3 times,
k2 tog, yrn, p2, k2.
Rib 17 rows.
Buttonhole row Rib 24(28:36:40), [k2 tog, yrn, rib 10] 3 times,
k2 tog, yrn, p2, k2.
Rib 3 rows.
Cast off in rib.

NECK EDGING

Join shoulder seams.
With right side facing, starting at beg of neck shaping,
using 4.50mm (US 7) needles and yarn double, pick up and
k14(15:17:18) sts up right side of front neck, 22(24:24:26) sts
from back neck, pick up and k14(15:17:18) sts down left side
of front neck. 50(54:58:62) sts.
P 1 row.
Cast off.

SCARF

With 5mm (US 8) needles and yarn used double cast on
22(22:26:26) sts.
1st rib row K2, [p2, k2] to end.
2nd rib row P2, [k2, p2] to end.
These 2 rows form the rib.
Continue in rib until scarf measures 90(90:100:100)cm/
35 ½(35 ½:39 ½:39 ½)in from cast on edge.
Cast off in rib.

TO MAKE UP

Join side and sleeve seams. Sew in sleeves. Sew on buttons.
Fold scarf so that one 'half' is 10cm/4in longer than other half,
with fold to centre of back neck and longer half on right front,
sew scarf to neck edging.

LOVISA CARDIGAN

SKILL LEVEL **Beginner / Improving**

SIZES / MEASUREMENTS

To fit age	2-3	3-4	4-5	5-6	years

ACTUAL GARMENT MEASUREMENTS

Chest	56	61	66	70	cm
	22	24	26	27 ½	in
Length to	36	40	45	51	cm
shoulder	14	15 ¾	17 ¾	20	in
Sleeve length	16	18	20	22	cm
with cuff folded back	6 ¼	7	8	8 ¾	in

MATERIALS

3(3:4:5) 50g/1 ¾oz balls of MillaMia Naturally Soft Merino in Storm (102) (A).
3(3:4:4) balls of Putty Grey (121) (B).
1(1:2:2) balls of Fuchsia (143) (C).
Pair each of 3mm (US 2) and 3.25mm (US 3) needles.
One large button (approx 23mm/⅞in diameter) and two smaller buttons (approx 18mm/¾in diameter).

TENSION / GAUGE

25 sts and 34 rows to 10cm/4in square over st st using 3.25 mm (US 3) needles.

HINTS AND TIPS

Choose fun contrast colours for the sleeve bands and button bands to bring the design to life. Note that the decreases for the front neck and armhole are worked **at the same time** on the fronts.

ABBREVIATIONS

See page 9.

SUGGESTED ALTERNATIVE COLOURWAYS

Plum 162	Fawn 160	Claret 104	Seaside 161	Forget me not 120	Midnight 101	Fuchsia 143	Petal 122	Daisy Yellow 142

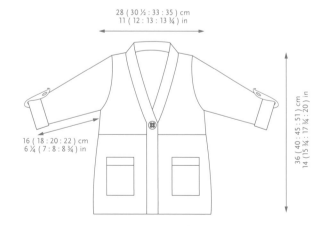

28 (30 ½ : 33 : 35) cm
11 (12 : 13 : 13 ¾) in

16 (18 : 20 : 22) cm
6 ¼ (7 : 8 : 8 ¾) in

36 (40 : 45 : 51) cm
14 (15 ¾ : 17 ¾ : 20) in

BACK

With 3.25mm (US 3) needles and A cast on 95(103:111:119) sts.
Cont in g-st until back measures 20(22:26:30)cm/8(8 ¾:10 ¼:
11 ¾)in from cast on edge, ending with a right side row.
Dec row P2, [p2 tog, p2] 22(24:26:28) times, p2 tog, p3.
72(78:84:90) sts.
Change to B.
Beg with a k row cont in st st until back measures 24(27:31:36)cm/
9 ½(10 ½:12 ¼:14)in from cast on edge, ending with a wrong
side row.
Shape armholes
Cast off 4(5:6:7) sts at beg of next 2 rows. 64(68:72:76) sts.
Next row K2, skpo, k to last 4 sts, k2 tog, k2.
Next row P to end.
Rep the last 2 rows 6 times more. 50(54:58:62) sts.
Cont in st st until back measures 36(40:45:51)cm/14(15 ¾:
17 ¾:20)in from cast on edge, ending with a wrong side row.
Shape shoulders
Cast off 5(6:6:7) sts at the beg of next 2 rows and 5(5:6:6) sts
at beg of foll 2 rows. 30(32:34:36) sts
Cast off.

LEFT FRONT

With 3.25mm (US 3) needles and A cast on 45(49:53:57) sts.
Cont in g-st until front measures 20(22:26:30)cm/8(8 ¾:10 ¼:
11 ¾)in from cast on edge, ending with a right side row.
Dec row P1, [p2 tog, p2] 11(12:13:14) times. 34(37:40:43) sts.
Change to B and st st.
Shape front neck
1st row K to last 4 sts, k2 tog, k2.
Work 3 rows.
Dec one st at neck edge on the next and 11(12:13:14) foll 4th
rows **at the same time** when front measures 24(27:31:36)cm/
9 ½(10 ½:12 ¼:14)in from cast on edge, ending with a wrong
side row, **shape armhole** as follows:
Next row Cast off 4(5:6:7) sts, k to end.

Next row P to end.
Next row K2, skpo, k to end.
Next row P to end.
Dec one st at armhole edge on next 6 right side rows.
When all neck decs have been worked cont straight until front
measures the same as back to shoulder shaping,
ending at armhole edge.
Shape shoulder
Next row Cast off 5(6:6:7) sts, k to end.
P 1 row.
Cast off rem 5(5:6:6) sts.

RIGHT FRONT

With 3.25mm (US 3) needles and A cast on 45(49:53:57) sts.
Cont in g-st until front measures 20(22:26:30)cm/8(8 ¾:10 ¼:11 ¾)in
from cast on edge, ending with a right side row.
Dec row [P2 tog, p2] 11(12:13:14) times, p1. 34(37:40:43) sts.
Change to B and st st.
Shape front neck
1st row K2, skpo, k to end.
Work 3 rows.
Dec one st at neck edge on the next and 11(12:13:14) foll 4th
rows **at the same time** when front measures 24(27:31:36)cm/
9 ½(10 ½:12 ¼:14)in from cast on edge, ending with a right
side row, **shape armhole** as follows:
Next row Cast off 4(5:6:7) sts, p to end.
Next row K to last 4 sts, k2 tog, k2.
Next row P to end.
Dec one st at armhole edge on next 6 right side rows.
When all neck decs have been worked cont straight until front
measures the same as back to shoulder shaping,
ending at armhole edge.
Shape shoulder
Next row Cast off 5(6:6:7) sts, p to end.
K 1 row.
Cast off rem 5(5:6:6) sts.

POCKETS (make 2)

With 3.25mm (US 3) needles and A cast on 24(28:28:32) sts.
Beg with a k row work 8(9:9:10)cm/3(3 ½:3 ½:4)in in g-st,
ending with a wrong side row.
Change to C.
K 1 row.
1st row P to end.
2nd row K3, [p2, k2] to last 5 sts, p2, k3.
Rep the last 2 rows 2(3:3:4) times more, and then the 1st row
again.
Cast off in rib.

SLEEVES

With 3mm (US 2) needles and A cast on 60(66:72:78) sts.
Cont in g-st until cuff measures 6(6:7:7)cm/2 ½(2 ½:2 ¾:2 ¾)in
from cast on edge.
Change to B.
Mark each end of last row with a coloured thread.
Beg with a k row cont in st st until sleeve measures
10(10:11:11)cm/4(4:4 ¼:4 ¼)in from coloured thread, ending
with a p row.
Change to 3.25mm (US 3) needles.
Cont in st st until sleeve measures 16(18:20:22)cm/6 ¼(7:8:8 ¾)in
from coloured thread, ending with a p row.
Shape top
Cast off 4(5:6:7) sts at beg of next 2 rows. 52(56:60:64) sts.
Next row K2, skpo, k to last 4 sts, k2 tog, k2.
Next row P to end.
Next row K to end.
Next row P to end.
Rep the last 4 rows 0(1:2:3) times. 50(52:54:56) sts.
Next row K2, skpo, k to last 4 sts, k2 tog, k2.
Next row P to end.
Rep the last 2 rows 8 times more. 32(34:36:38) sts.
Cast off 3 sts at beg of next 8 rows.
Cast off rem 8(10:12:14) sts.

FRONTBAND

With 3mm (US 2) needles and C cast on 13 sts.
1st row [P1, k2] 3 times, p1, k3.
2nd row P to end.
Rep the last 2 rows until band, when slightly stretched fits up
right front to beg of neck shaping.
Buttonhole row P1, k2, p1, k2 tog, y2rn, skpo, k1, p1, k3.
Cont in patt until band fits up remainder of right front across
back neck and down left front.
Cast off.

SLEEVE BANDS (make 2)

With 3mm (US 2) needles and C cast on 13 sts.
1st row P1, [k2, p1] 4 times.
2nd row P to end.
Rep the last 2 rows until band measures 12(12:14:14)cm/
4 ¾(4 ¾:5 ½:5 ½)in from cast on edge, ending with a p row.
Next row P1, skpo, patt to last 3 sts, k2 tog, p1.
Next row P to end.
Rep the last 2 rows 3 times more. 5 sts.
Next row P1, s1 1, k2 tog, psso, p1. 3 sts.
Next row P to end.
P3 tog.
Fasten off.

TO MAKE UP

Join side and sleeve seams, reversing seam on cuffs to fold
back. Sew on sleeves. Sew on pockets. Fold back cuffs. Place
sleeve bands around cuff and sew cast on edge to wrong side
on sleeves and secure in place on right side with a button. Sew
on buttons.

From left to right:
Sebastian Jumper
in Grass (141) and
in Midnight (101)
pattern on page 98

SEBASTIAN
JUMPER

SEBASTIAN JUMPER

SKILL LEVEL **Experienced**

SIZES / MEASUREMENTS

To fit age	1-2	3-4	5-6	7-8	years

ACTUAL GARMENT MEASUREMENTS

Chest	57	64	70	76	cm
	22 ½	25	27 ½	30	in
Length to	33	39	45	53	cm
shoulder	13	15 ½	17 ¾	21	in
Sleeve	19	23	28	33	cm
length	7 ½	9	11	13	in

MATERIALS

5 (6:7:8) 50g balls of MillaMia Naturally Soft Merino in Midnight (101).
Pair each of 3mm (US 2) and 3.25mm (US 3) needles.
6 small buttons (approx 13mm/½in diameter).

TENSION / GAUGE

25 sts and 34 rows to 10cm/4in square over st st using 3.25mm (US 3) needles.

HINTS AND TIPS

At last an everyday versatile boy's sweater. Be aware that there is some short row shaping in the collar to give it some added volume. Remember when sewing up the side seams to leave a gap at the bottom for the side vents.

ABBREVIATIONS

See page 9.

SUGGESTED ALTERNATIVE COLOURWAYS

Grass	Seaside	Scarlet	Forget me not	Peacock
141	161	140	120	144

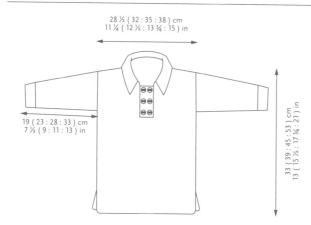

28 ½ (32 : 35 : 38) cm
11 ¼ (12 ½ : 13 ¾ : 15) in

19 (23 : 28 : 33) cm
7 ½ (9 : 11 : 13) in

33 (39 : 45 : 53) cm
13 (15 ½ : 17 ¾ : 21) in

BACK

With 3mm (US 2) needles cast on 74(82:90:98) sts.
1st row [P1, k2] twice, p1, [k4, p4] to last 11 sts, k4, [p1, k2] twice, p1.
2nd row P to end.
Rep the last 2 rows 4 times more.
Change to 3.25mm (US 3) needles.
1st row [P1, k2] twice, p1, k to last 7 sts, [p1, k2] twice, p1.
2nd row P to end.
Rep the last 2 rows 4 times more.
Beg with a k row cont in st st until back measures 33(39:45:53)cm/
13(15 ½:17 ¾:21)in from cast on edge, ending with a p row.
Shape shoulders
Cast off 6(7:8:9) sts at beg of next 4 rows and 7(8:9:10) sts at
beg of foll 2 rows.
Leave rem 36(38:40:42) sts on a holder.

FRONT

Work as given for back until front measures 20(24:28:34)cm/
8(9 ½:11:13 ½)in from cast on edge, ending with a k row.
Front opening
Next row P42(46:50:54) turn and work on these sts for right front.
Next row P1, [k2, p1] 3 times, k32(36:40:44).
Next row P to end.
Rep the last 2 rows until 20(20:22:22) rows less have been
worked than on back to shoulder shaping, ending with a p row.
Shape front neck
Next row Patt 14(15:15:16), leave these sts on a holder, k to end.
Next row P to end.
Next row K1, skpo, k to end.
Rep the last 2 rows 8(8:9:9) times more. 19(22:25:28) sts.
Work 2 rows.
Shape shoulder
Cast off 6(7:8:9) sts at beg of next and foll wrong side row.
Work 1 row.
Cast off rem 7(8:9:10) sts.

Mark positions for buttons, the first pair on the 3rd row of
buttonband, the third pair 2 rows below neck shaping and one
pair spaced evenly between.
Second side
Cast on 10 sts, then with wrong side facing, p across sts on left
front. 42(46:50:54) sts.
Next row K32(36:40:44), p1, [k2, p1] 3 times, turn and work on
these sts for left front.
Next row P to end.
Next row K32(36:40:44), p1, k2 tog, yrn, p1, k2, p1, yon, skpo, p1.
Next row P to end.
Cont as set, working buttonholes to match markers until
21(21:23:23) rows less have been worked than on back to
shoulder shaping, ending with a right side row.
Shape front neck
Next row P14(15:15:16) sts, leave these sts on a holder, p to end.
Next row K to last 3 sts, k2 tog, k1.
Next row P to end.
Rep the last 2 rows 8(8:9:9) times more. 19(22:25:28) sts.
Work 2 rows.
Shape shoulder
Cast off 6(7:8:9) sts at beg of next and foll right side row.
Work 1 row.
Cast off rem 7(8:9:10) sts.

SLEEVES

With 3mm (US 2) needles cast on 42(50:58:66) sts.
1st row K3, [p4, k4] to last 7 sts, p4, k3.
2nd row P3, [k4, p4] to last 7 sts, k4, p3.
Rep the last 2 rows 5(6:7:8) times more.
Change to 3.25mm (US 3) needles and beg with a k row cont in st st.
Work 6(6:8:10) rows.
Inc row K3, m1, k to last 3 sts, m1, k3.
Work 5(7:9:11) rows.
Rep the last 6(8:10:12) rows 5 times more, and then the inc row again. 56(64:72:80) sts.
Cont straight until sleeve measures 19(23:28:33)cm/
7 ½(9:11:13)in from cast on edge, ending with a p row.
Cast off.

COLLAR

Join shoulder seams.
With 3mm (US 2) needles and right side facing, slip 14(15:15:16) sts from right front onto a needle, pick up and k21(22:24:25) sts up right front, k36(38:40:42) sts from back neck holder, pick up and k21(22:24:25) sts down left side of front neck, patt 14(15:15:16) from left front holder. 106(112:118:124) sts.
Cont in rib patt as set by front bands.
Next 2 rows P to last 30(30:36:36) sts, turn, patt to last 30(30:36:36) sts, turn.
Next 2 rows P to last 24(24:30:30) sts, turn, patt to last 24(24:30:30) sts, turn.
Next 2 rows P to last 18(18:24:24) sts, turn, patt to last 18(18:24:24) sts, turn.
3rd and 4th sizes only
Next 2 rows P to last −(-:18:18) sts, turn, patt to last −(-:18:18) sts, turn.
All sizes
Next row Cast off 6 sts, p to end.
Next row Cast off 6 sts, 1 st rem on right hand needle, [k2, p1] to end.
Change to 3.25mm (US 3) needles and reverse the patt.
Next row P1, [k2, p1] to end.
Next row Patt to end.
Rep the last 2 rows 10(11:11:12) times more, and then the 1st row again.
Cast off loosely in rib.

TO MAKE UP

Lap right front border behind left and sew cast on edge of left front border at centre front. Sew on sleeves. Join side (to top of rib, leaving vent open) and sleeve seams. Sew on buttons.

From left to right: **Lina Dress** in Lilac Blossom (123) and Storm (102) pattern on page 108 and **Lilian Jacket** in Lilac Blossom (123) and Storm (102) pattern on page 104

LILIAN
JACKET
LINA
DRESS

LILIAN JACKET

SKILL LEVEL **Beginner**

SIZES / MEASUREMENTS

To fit age	0-3	6-12	12-18	18-24	24-36	36-48	mths

ACTUAL GARMENT MEASUREMENTS

Chest	48	52	56	58	64	68	cm
	19	20 ½	22	23	25	27	in
Length to	23	25	28	31	34	38	cm
shoulder	9	10	11	12 ¼	13 ¼	15	in
Sleeve length	9	11	13	15	18	20	cm
with cuff folded back	3 ½	4 ¼	5	6	7	8	in

MATERIALS

3 (4:5:5:6:6) 50g/1 ¾oz balls of MillaMia Naturally Soft Merino in Lilac Blossom (123) (M).
1 (1:1:1:2:2) balls of contrast Storm (102) (C).
Pair each of 3mm (US 2) and 3.25mm (US 3) knitting needles.
46cm/18in long ribbon (approx 1.5cm/⅜in wide).

TENSION / GAUGE

25 sts and 50 rows to 10cm/4in square over g-st using 3.25mm (US 3) needles.

HINTS AND TIPS

Super simple yet effective this looks so sweet with the simple ribbon tie. Ideal for beginner knitters in garter stitch throughout and with minimal shaping, the border is not sewn on but knitted in. Make sure you twist your yarn on the wrong side of the work when you are changing the yarn colours for the border. It actually also looks great worn as a small fit on older girls – as seen on page 4.

ABBREVIATIONS

See page 9

SUGGESTED ALTERNATIVE COLOURWAYS

| Fuchsia 143 | Daisy Yellow 142 | Snow 124 | Forget me not 120 | Midnight 101 | Forget me not 120 | Petal 122 | Putty Grey 121 |

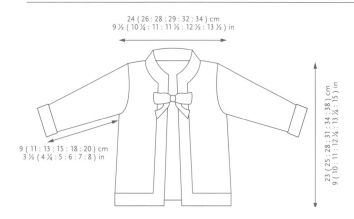

24 (26 : 28 : 29 : 32 : 34) cm
9 ½ (10 ¼ : 11 : 11 ½ : 12 ½ : 13 ½) in

9 (11 : 13 : 15 : 18 : 20) cm
3 ½ (4 ¼ : 5 : 6 : 7 : 8) in

23 (25 : 28 : 31 : 34 : 38) cm
9 (10 : 11 : 12 ¼ : 13 ¼ : 15) in

BACK

With 3mm (US 2) needles and C cast on 61(67:71:75:81:87) sts.
K11(11:13:13:15:15) rows.
Break off C.
Join on M.
Change to 3.25mm (US 3) needles.
Work in g-st until back measures 13(14:16:18:20:23)cm/5(5 ½: 6 ¼:7:8:9)in from cast on edge, ending with a wrong side row.
Shape armholes
Cast off 4 sts at beg of next 2 rows. 53(59:63:67:73:79) sts.
Next row K2, skpo, k to last 4 sts, k2 tog, k2.
Next row K to end.
Rep the last 2 rows 1(2:2:2:3:4) times. 49(53:57:61:65:69) sts.
Cont straight until back measures 23(25:28:31:34:38)cm/
9(10:11:12 ¼:13 ¼:15)in from cast on edge, ending with a wrong side row.
Shape shoulders
Cast off 11(12:13:14:15:16) sts at beg of next 2 rows.
Leave rem 27(29:31:33:35:37) sts on a holder.

LEFT FRONT

With 3mm (US 2) needles and C cast on 31(34:36:38:41:44) sts.
K11(11:13:13:15:15) rows.
Break off C.
Join on M.
Change to 3.25mm (US 3) needles.
Next row (right side) With M, k to last 6(6:7:7:8:8) sts, join on C, k6(6:7:7:8:8)C.
Next row K6(6:7:7:8:8)C, with M k to end.
These 2 rows form the g-st with contrast border patt.
Work straight until front measures 13(14:16:18:20:23)cm/
5(5 ½:6 ¼:7:8:9)in from cast on edge, ending with a wrong side row.
Shape armhole
Cast off 4 sts at beg of next row. 27(30:32:34:37:40) sts.
Next row Patt to end.
Next row K2, skpo, patt to end.
Rep the last 2 rows 1(2:2:2:3:4) times. 25(27:29:31:33:35) sts.
Work straight until front measures 19(21:23:26:28:32)cm/
7 ½(8 ¼:9:10 ¼:11:12 ½)in from cast on edge, ending with a wrong side row.
Shape neck
Next row K to last 6(7:8:9:10:11) sts, leave these sts on a holder.
Next row K to end.
Next row K to last 4 sts, k2 tog, k2.
Rep the last 2 rows until 11(12:13:14:15:16) sts rem.
Cont straight until front measures same as back to shoulder, ending at armhole edge.
Shape shoulder
Cast off.

RIGHT FRONT

With 3mm (US 2) needles and C cast on 31(34:36:38:41:44) sts.
K11(11:13:13:15:15) rows.
Change to 3.25mm (US 3) needles.
Next row (right side) K6(6:7:7:8:8)C, join on M, k to end.
Next row With M, k to last 6(6:7:7:8:8) sts, k6(6:7:7:8:8)C.
These 2 rows form the g-st with contrast border patt.
Work straight until front measures 13(14:16:18:20:23)cm/
5(5 ½:6 ¼:7:8:9)in from cast on edge, ending with a
right side row.
Shape armhole
Cast off 4 sts at beg of next row. 27(30:32:34:37:40) sts.
Next row Patt to last 4 sts, k2 tog, k2.
Next row Patt to end.
Rep the last 2 rows 1(2:2:2:3:4) times. 25(27:29:31:33:35) sts.
Work straight until front measures 19(21:23:26:28:32)cm/
7 ½(8 ¼:9:10 ¼:11:12 ½)in from cast on edge, ending with a
wrong side row.
Shape neck
Next row K6(7:8:9:10:11)C, leave these 6(7:8:9:10:11) sts on a
holder, then with M, k to end.
Next row K to end.
Next row K2, skpo, k to end.
Rep the last 2 rows until 11(12:13:14:15:16) sts rem.
Cont straight until front measures same as back to shoulder,
ending at armhole edge.
Shape shoulder
Cast off.

SLEEVES

With 3.25mm (US 3) needles and M cast on 27(29:33:35:39:41) sts.
K15(17:17:19:19:21) rows.
Mark each end of last row with a coloured thread.
Change to 3mm (US 2) needles.
K a further 15(17:17:19:19:21) rows.

Change to 3.25mm (US 3) needles.
Beg with a k row, cont in g-st.
Work 4(6:6:2:2:2) rows.
Inc row K3, m1, k to last 3 sts, m1, k3.
Work 3(3:3:5:5:5) rows.
Rep the last 4(4:4:6:6:6) rows 4(5:7:8:10:11) times more, and
then the inc row again. 39(43:51:55:63:67) sts.
Cont straight until sleeve measures 9(11:13:15:18:20)cm/
3 ½(4 ¼:5:6:7:8)in from coloured thread, ending with a right
side row.
Shape sleeve top
Cast off 4 sts at beg of next 2 rows. 31(35:43:47:55:59) sts.
Next row K2, skpo, k to last 4 sts, k2 tog, k2.
K 3 rows.
Rep the last 4 rows 6(7:8:9:10:11) times.
17(19:25:27:33:35) sts.
Cast off 2 sts at beg of next 4(4:6:6:8:8) rows.
Cast off.

NECKBAND

Join shoulder seams.
With right side facing and 3mm (US 2) needles and C, slip
6(7:8:9:10:11) sts from right front neck holder onto a needle,
pick up and k16(16:17:17:18:18) sts up right front neck,
k27(29:31:33:35:37) sts from back neck holder, pick up and
k16(16:17:17:18:18) sts down left front neck, k6(7:8:9:10:11) sts
from left front holder. 71(75:81:85:91:95) sts.
K11(11:13:13:15:15) rows.
Cast off.

TO MAKE UP

Join side and sleeve seams (reversing seam on foldback for
cuffs). Sew in sleeves. Cut ribbon in half, sew one piece to
each front on underside of border.

LINA DRESS

SKILL LEVEL **Improving**

SIZES / MEASUREMENTS

To fit age	1-2	2-3	4-5	5-6	years

ACTUAL GARMENT MEASUREMENTS

Chest	58	62	67	72	cm
	23	24 ½	26 ½	28 ½	in
Length to	51	56	62	70	cm
shoulder	20	22	24 ½	27 ½	in
Sleeve	1 ½	1 ½	1 ½	1 ½	cm
length	¾	¾	¾	¾	in

MATERIALS

5(6:6:7) 50g/1 ¾oz balls of MillaMia Naturally Soft Merino in Lilac Blossom (123) (M).
2 balls of Storm (102) (C).
Pair each of 3mm (US 2) and 3.25mm (US 3) needles.
130cm/51 ¼in long ribbon (approx 1.5cm/⅜in wide).

TENSION / GAUGE

25 sts and 34 rows to 10cm/4in square over st st using 3.25mm (US 3) needles.

HINTS AND TIPS

Soft and welcoming in muted pastel shades or try it in darker contrast colours for a bolder statement. Midnight and Snow will produce an on-trend nautical look.

ABBREVIATIONS

See page 9.

SUGGESTED ALTERNATIVE COLOURWAYS

Plum	Fawn	Petal	Putty Grey	Midnight	Snow
162	160	122	121	101	124

29 (31 : 33 ½ : 36) cm
11 ½ (12 ¼ : 13 ¼ : 14 ¼) in

51 (56 : 62 : 70) cm
20 (22 : 24 ½ : 27 ½) in

BACK and FRONT (alike)

With 3.25mm (US 3) needles and C cast on 98(110:122:134) sts.
1st row P2, [k4, p2] to end.
2nd row K2, [p4, k2] to end.
Rep the last 2 rows twice more.
Change to M.
Beg with a k row cont in st st.
Work 2 rows.
Dec row K4, skpo, k to last 6 sts, k2 tog, k4.
Work 5 rows.
Rep the last 6 rows 10(13:16:19) times more, and then the dec row again. 74(80:86:92) sts.
Work straight until back measures 25(29:34:41)cm/10(11 ½: 13 ½:16)in from cast on edge, ending with a wrong side row.
Change to C.
Work a further 8 rows.
Work eyelet openings:
K14(16:18:20), turn, [k1, p to end, k14(16:18:20), turn] 3 times, break off yarn, rejoin yarn to next st, k4, turn, [k1, p2, k1, turn, k4, turn] 3 times, break off yarn, rejoin yarn to next st, k38(40:42:44), turn, [k1, p36(38:40:42), k1, turn, k38(40:42:44), turn] 3 times, break off yarn, rejoin yarn to next st, k4, turn, [k1, p2, k1, turn, k4, turn] 3 times, break off yarn, rejoin yarn to next st, k14(16:18:20), turn, [p13(15:16:19), k1, turn, k to end] 3 times.
Next row P across all sts.
Work a further 8 rows.
Change to M.
Beg with a k row cont in st st until back measures 35(39:44:51)cm/13 ¾(15 ½:17 ½:20)in from cast on edge, ending with a wrong side row.
Shape armholes
Cast off 4(5:6:7) sts at beg of next 2 rows. 66(70:74:78) sts.
Next row K4, skpo, k to last 6 sts, k2 tog, k4.
Next row P to end.
Rep the last 2 rows 17(18:19:20) times more. 30(32:34:36) sts.
Leave these sts on a spare needle.

SLEEVES

With 3mm (US 2) needles and C cast on 56(62:68:74) sts.
1st row P2, [k4, p2] to end.
2nd row K2, [p4, k2] to end.
Rep the last 2 rows twice more.
Change to 3.25mm (US 3) needles.
Cont in stripes of 2 rows M and 2 rows C.
Shape top
Cast off 4(5:6:7) sts at beg of next 2 rows. 48(52:56:60) sts.
Next row K4, skpo, k to last 6 sts, k2 tog, k4.
Next row P to end.
Next row K to end.
Next row P to end.
Rep the last 4 rows 5 times more. 36(40:44:48) sts.
Next row K4, skpo, k to last 6 sts, k2 tog, k4.
Next row P to end.
Rep the last 2 rows 5(6:7:8) times. 24(26:28:30) sts.
Leave these sts on a spare needle.

NECKBAND

With 3mm (US 2) needles, right side facing, and C, k23(25:27:29) from left sleeve, k last st tog with first st on front, k28(30:32:34), k last st tog with first st on right sleeve, k22(24:26:28), k last st tog with first st on back, k14(15:16:17), m1, k15(16:17:18). 106(114:122:130) sts.
1st row K2, [p2, k2] to end.
2nd row P2, [k2, p2] to end.
Rep the last 2 rows once more, and then the 1st row again.
Cast off in rib.

TO MAKE UP

Join raglan seams.
Join side and sleeve seams. Thread ribbon through loops to tie at front.

YARN COLOURS

Midnight
101

Storm
102

Moss
103

Claret
104

Forget
me not
120

Putty Grey
121

Petal
122

Lilac
Blossom
123

Snow
124

Scarlet
140

Grass
141

Daisy
Yellow
142

Fuchsia
143

Peacock
144

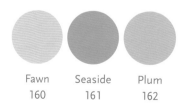

Fawn
160

Seaside
161

Plum
162

NOTES

INDEX

KLARA KIMONO
page 60

FILIPPA DRESS
page 66

FILIP TANK TOP
page 72

FIA HAT & SCARF
page 78

CISSI SWING COAT
page 86

LOVISA CARDIGAN
page 92

SEBASTIAN JUMPER
page 98

LILIAN JACKET
page 104

LINA DRESS
page 108

ABOUT MILLAMIA

When we launched with our first two books, The Close Knit Gang and Bright Young Things, we did so based on a hunch that there would be other people like us out there. People that loved knitting and also loved modern design. It has been so rewarding to discover that our hunch was correct, and that you are now asking for more of our designs.

Since our launch we have been privileged enough to meet many of you at various events – either knitting shows, yarn shop visits or press occasions. It is always exciting for us when customers recognise the MillaMia product. Even better is that we have gotten to know many of you personally in this way too.

Many of you have given us feedback directly when we meet, or via our Facebook and Twitter pages. As such we have really been able to adapt the collection in this book to what you have told us. You mentioned you wanted patterns for older children – well in this book we have extended the grading on some of our patterns to accommodate this. You can now knit many of our designs up to the ages of 6, 7 and 8 years. Also you requested more strong items for boys – with an active 3 year old boy in the family we also wanted this, and we are really proud of the boys' items in this book.

In this collection it was important for us to stay true to what you told us you loved about our first two books. The fresh, modern design. The fact that our patterns are different from what is available already. Our use of colour and the colour combinations that are put together. We hope you agree that while refreshingly new, the patterns contained on the preceding pages are true MillaMia designs!

We are excited about the future – we have had lots of requests for us to start offering adult patterns and these are our next priority. The fact that you love knitting with our yarn and repeatedly tell us this has really spurred us on, as with adult patterns added to our range we believe we can inspire yet more knitters.

Thank you for your on-going support. We could not be happier with how MillaMia is growing – available now internationally and sold in lots of shops which we hope makes it easier for you to stock up for your next projects.

Finally we also wanted to introduce Kirsten to you. A friend who has now become an intrinsic part of MillaMia during the course of the last year. Helping us with everything from sales to strategy and representing us in Australasia, she has quickly become a core member of our team.

As ever – please let us know if you have any other feedback or comments. We hope you can tell that we really do listen to it and value your opinions.

With best wishes,

Katarina and Helena Rosén
katarina@millamia.com or helena@millamia.com